SECRETS TO SAFETY

HOME INVASION PROTECTION AND PERSONAL DEFENSE

20 Year Veteran Law Enforcement Officer

State Certified Instructor for Law Enforcement

ALVIN "GOLDIE" MACK Ph.D.

1st printing   © Copyright – 2019   Printed in U.S.A. 2019.

Arts East Publishing House

SECRETS TO SAFETY

SECRETS TO SAFETY Written by Alvin "Goldie" Mack Ph.D.
Published by Arts East Publishing House

1st printing © Copyright – 2019   Printed in U.S.A. 2019.

Dedicated to

My family for all their support that they have given me throughout the years.

A special thank you to Jana Sanders for your encouragement and devotion through trying times.

SECRETS TO SAFETY

TABLE OF CONTENTS

INTRODUCTION 5

CHAPTER 1 11

Some facts about home invasion

CHAPTER 2 30

Is Anyone home?

CHAPTER 3 39

Play by the rules

CHAPTER 4 70

The real truth about rape

CHAPTER 5 96

Self Defense that works

CHAPTER 6 128

Understanding trauma

CHAPTER 7 139

The after effects

CHAPTER 8 154

Stages of adjustment

ABOUT THE AUTHOR 162

LETTERS OF RECOMENDATION 166

INTRODUCTION

W hen a crowd rushes into your house without declaring its intention, it is, by definition, an invasion.

Viktor Orban

In some parts of the United States and some other English-speaking countries, home invasion is an illegal and usually forceful entry to an occupied, private dwelling with intent to commit a violent crime against the occupants, such as robbery, assault, rape, murder, or kidnapping.

SECRETS TO SAFETY

In some jurisdictions, there is a defined crime of home invasion; in others, there is no crime defined as home invasion, but events that accompany the invasion are charged as crimes. Where home invasion is defined, the definition and punishments vary by jurisdiction.

It is not a legally defined federal offense throughout the United States but it is in several states, such as Georgia, Michigan, Connecticut, Illinois, Florida, Louisiana, and Nevada. Home invasion laws also have been introduced in the South Carolina General Assembly and in the State of Maryland. On March 15, 2011, a bill making home invasion deaths a capital crime in New Hampshire passed the New Hampshire House without debate. Home invasion as such is not defined as a crime in most countries other than the US, with offenders being charged according to the actual crimes committed once inside the building, such as armed robbery, rape or murder. In English law, offenders who commit burglary while carrying a weapon can be convicted of the offense of aggravated burglary even if the weapon is not actually brandished or used.

Home invasion differs from burglary in that its perpetrators have a violent intent apart from the unlawful entry itself, specific or general, much the same way as aggravated robbery—personally taking from someone by force—is differentiated from mere larceny (theft alone).

The first published use of the term "home invasion" recorded in the Oxford English Dictionary is an article in The Washington Post on 1 February 1912, with an article in the Los Angeles Times on 18 March 1925 clearly indicating the modern meaning.

"Home-invasion robberies" were highlighted in June 1995, when the term appeared in the cover story of The FBI Law Enforcement Bulletin in an article written by Police Chief James T. Hurley of the Ft. Lauderdale, Florida, area, later republished on BNET the online blog posted by Harvard Business School. Hurley posted that, at the time, the crime could be considered an alternative to bank or convenience store robberies, which were becoming more difficult to carry out due to technological advances in security. In the same article, Hurley recommended educating the public about home invasion. Before the term "home invasion" came in use, the term "hot burglary" was often used in the literature. Early references also use "burglary of occupied homes" and "burglar striking an occupied residence".

Connecticut Congressman Chris Murphy proposed in 2008 making home invasion a federal crime in the United States.

One well-known home invasion is November 15, 1959, quadruple murder of the Clutter family by Richard "Dick" Hickock and Perry Edward Smith during a home-invasion robbery in rural Holcomb, Kansas. The murders were detailed in Truman Capote's "nonfiction novel" In Cold Blood. However, the perpetrators were convicted of murder, not home invasion.

More recently, two paroled criminals were each charged with three counts of capital murder during a home invasion into the Petit family home in Cheshire, Connecticut, on July 23, 2007. During the invasion, the mother died of asphyxiation due to strangulation and the two daughters died of smoke inhalation after the suspects set the house on fire. The men were charged with first-degree sexual assault, the murder of a kidnapped person, and murder of two or more people at the same time. The state attorney sought the death penalty against the suspects. The first defendant, Steven Hayes, was found guilty of 16 of the 17 counts including capital murder on October 5, 2010, and on November 8, 2010, was sentenced to death. His co-defendant, Joshua Komisarjevsky, was convicted of all 17 counts against him in October 2011 and was also sentenced to death. Both men later had their sentences commuted to life without parole when Connecticut abolished the death penalty in 2015.

Another home invasion occurred on November 26, 2007, when Washington Redskins star Sean Taylor was murdered during an overnight home invasion of his suburban Miami home. Four defendants were charged with this crime.

Many U.S. states (particularly those that endorse the Castle Doctrine) include defending oneself against forcible entry of one's home as part of their definition of justifiable homicide without any obligation to retreat.

SO! Is your home a safe place for you and your family or does it send an open invitation to criminals?

I have been a police officer for over 20 years both in Fort Worth Texas, Denton Texas and Wichita Kansas I'm a former member of the president's anti-terrorism police task force and have been a martial arts instructor for over 50 years. I have noticed a very complacent attitude of both men and women about home safety particularly among African-Americans and Hispanics. I've been told it's something that happens, and no one can stop it. This revelation prompted me to start work on this book I believe that every person, man, woman and child should be able to handle themselves and should be physically and mentally able to take care of themselves when confronted.

This book was written for anyone who wants the skills to prevent becoming a victim of burglary and attack. Topics will include what is a home invasion, burglary and ways to protect themselves, their families and their home. This book should be shared with the whole family ages 6 and above. You will be taught to develop home safety plans in case you're ever at home when a home is broken into. Apartment dwellers also learn how to be safe in an apartment and also how to choose safety features when looking for an apartment. Readers will also be given the opportunity to learn how to receive up to 25% off their renters or homeowner's insurance.

Although some homeowners may consider putting bars on their doors and windows, sometimes that can be a detriment as opposed to being a safety factor. Especially in the case of fires where you are unable to get out of your home because you're restricted by the bars. I would suggest before you engage in baring up your windows, check before you purchase a home or rent an apartment. Go to your local law enforcement agency in any city and they will be able to provide you with crime statistics for that city. Where the highest crime rates are in a particular area whether that crime is car thefts, home burglaries, assaults etc. Make your decision on where you purchase your home or rent your apartment based on those factors.

Another thing that you may consider is to drive through communities and talk to some of the citizens that live in those communities. If you see a bunch of residences with bars all over the windows that may give you an indication on whether that is an area that you would like to live in whether you are renting or purchasing.

CHAPTER

Some Facts About Home Invasion

"It Can Happen to YOU!"

Household burglary - Unlawful or forcible entry or attempted entry of a residence. This crime usually, but not always, involves theft. The illegal entry may be by force, such as breaking a window or slashing a screen, or may be without force by entering through an unlocked door or an open window. As long as the person entering has no legal right to be present in the structure a burglary has occurred. Furthermore, the structure need not be the house itself for a burglary to take place; illegal entry of a garage, shed, or any other structure on the premises also constitutes household burglary. If breaking and entering occurs in a hotel or vacation residence, it is still classified as a burglary for the household whose member or members were staying there at the time the entry occurred. There is a difference between theft and burglary.

Theft is defined as: Taking of property with the intent to deprive the owner of the property, intentionally or knowingly, appropriates property (describe) by acquiring or otherwise exercising control of said property. (PC 31.03)

Burglary is defined as: With intent to commit a Felony or Theft intentionally or knowingly, without the effective consent of the owner, enters a habitation or building not then open to the public with intent to commit a felony, assault, or theft. (PC 30.02)

The chances of being burglarized are increasing every year. According to FBI statistics, a house, apartment or condominium is burglarized once every 15 seconds.

Burglary is probably the most preventable of crimes. Burglars look for what the police call "targets of opportunity" in other words, easy pickings. Whether you rent an apartment or condominium or own a home, there are a few simple precautions you can take to help protect yourself, your family, and your belongings. You can also talk to your landlord or building superintendent about increasing the security in and around your home.

A good security plan should include strong window, door, and lock products; good security habits and lifestyles. (for example, always locking doors at night or when the house is vacant: and natural surveillance, such as having neighborhood watches). Insurance can never replace keepsakes or priceless family heirlooms. And let's not forget about family security, not all burglars are just thieves.

Burglary, theft, and robbery each amount to billions of dollars in total monetary losses every year. Larceny-theft (or simply "theft") is defined as the unlawful removal of property. Burglary is defined as the unlawful entry into almost any structure with the intent to commit a crime inside. Robbery, on the other hand, is the violent theft of property or money.

CRIME TREND Rates of personal and household burglary, theft, and robbery have decreased consistently over the past two decades. The national rate of personal robbery has decreased 67%, from 6.3 victimizations per 1,000 people age 12 or older in 1995 to 2.1 per 1,000 in 2015. Similarly, the rate of personal theft dropped 84% (from 1.9 to 0.3), while burglary and household theft have declined 60% and 65%, respectively. The rate of motor vehicle theft has also declined 75% (from 17.1 to 4.3 per 1,000 households).

From 1995 to 2015, the rates of robbery, burglary, theft, and motor vehicle theft known to law enforcement have declined. Robbery has decreased from 2.2 per 1,000 individuals to 1. Burglary decreased 50%, from nearly 10 per 1,000 individuals to about 5. Similarly, larceny-theft and motor vehicle theft decreased by 41% and 61%, respectively. It is important to note that the Uniform Crime Report (UCR) includes commercial crimes in these estimates, while the National Crime Victimization Survey (NCVS) does not. Despite this difference, the UCR and NCVS have reported comparable changes over the years.

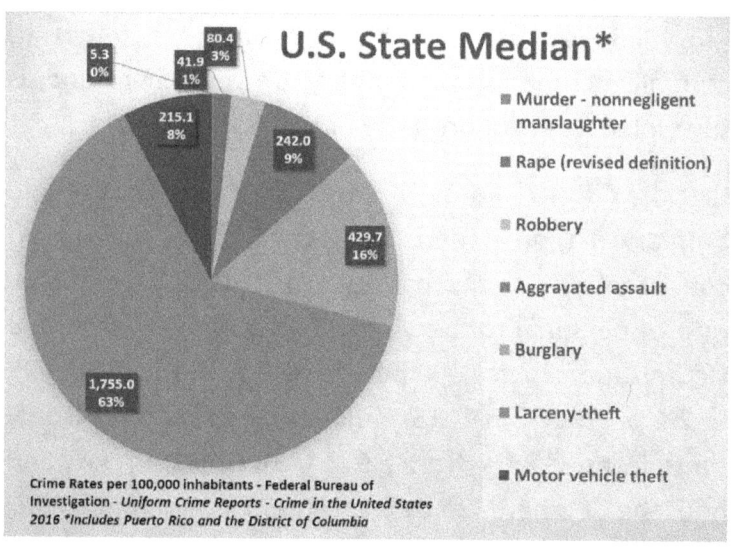

Crime Rates per 100,000 inhabitants - Federal Bureau of Investigation - *Uniform Crime Reports - Crime in the United States 2016 *Includes Puerto Rico and the District of Columbia*

In December 2017, a report listed the most common statistics for such crimes connected with home invasion or attack.

The stats of the home invasion crime statistics will keep you up at night

DID YOU KNOW?

In 2014, **60.9%** of robberies were reported to the **police.**^

In 2015, more than **50%** of robbery victimizations were committed by **strangers.**^

In 2015, 42% of robberies involved the use of **strong-arm** tactics, 41% involved the use of **firearms,** and 8% involved the use of a **knife** or other cutting instrument.[B4]

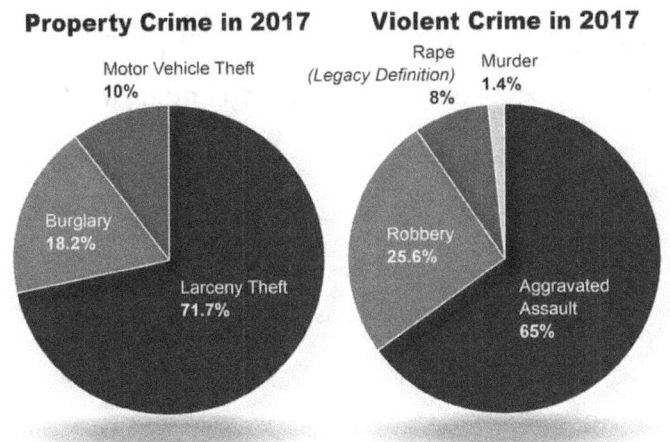

Property Crime in 2017

- Motor Vehicle Theft 10%
- Burglary 18.2%
- Larceny Theft 71.7%

Violent Crime in 2017

- Rape (Legacy Definition) 8%
- Murder 1.4%
- Robbery 25.6%
- Aggravated Assault 65%

From *Crime in the United States, 2017.*

SECRETS TO SAFETY

More often than not, this report focuses on FCRA compliant background checks and employee screening services designed to protect businesses from hiring the wrong people. But we're only at work for part of our lives and staying safe is a 24/7 job.

It's encouraging to note that instances of violent crime and property crime across the United States have been steadily trending down for well over a decade now. Of course, that doesn't mean crime is becoming rare. In fact, nearly 1 out of every 100 U.S. citizens over the age of 12 will become victims of crime at some point in their lives.

No, it's not pleasant to think about the possibility of becoming a victim to a violent crime. But hiding your head in the sand isn't going to help you or your loved ones either.

Below are updated statistics provided by U.S. government agencies for the period ending in 2016.

PROPERTY CRIME FACTS

According to the FBI, the U.S. Department of Justice, and other reputable sources, in the United States:

- One property crime happens every 4 seconds.

- One burglary occurs every 20 seconds.

- One violent crime occurs every 25 seconds.

- One aggravated assault occurs every 45 seconds.

- One robbery occurs every 90 seconds.

- One rape or attempted rape occurs every 5 minutes.

2017 CRIME STATISTICS

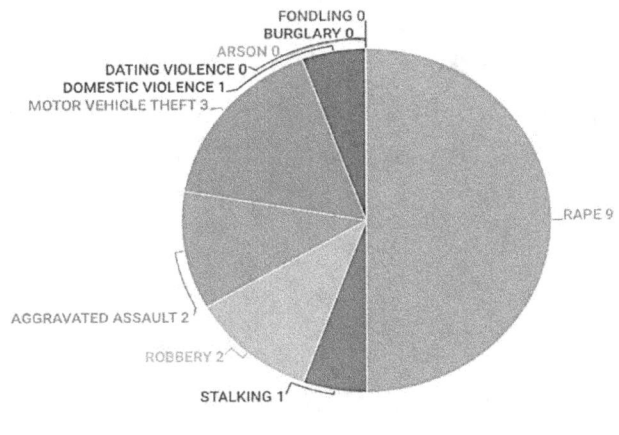

SECRETS TO SAFETY

- According to a United States Department of Justice report:

- 38% of assaults & 60% of rapes occur during home invasions.
- Over 2,000,000 homes will experience a break-in or burglary this year.

- There are over 4,500 home burglaries per day in the United States.

- The average number of home invasions per year was 1,030,000 between 1994 and 2010.

Whether it is workplace violence, home invasions, carjacking, armed robbery, rape, identity theft or any of a number of other crimes, YOU need to take control and arm yourself with the best available preventive measures.

DON'T BECOME JUST ANOTHER STATISTIC

One of these precautionary options is to make yourself aware of who you are dealing with through criminal background investigations, especially when inviting unknown people to do work in your home. Perform individual comprehensive background checks on the contractor and crew that you have hired to renovate your house, the plumber, your nanny, your new neighbor. You get the idea: if it doesn't feel right, it probably isn't, so it pays to know who and what you are dealing with. A search of national criminal records only takes a few days and costs very little, but the potential returns are priceless. Arm yourself with information and don't allow yourself to be blind-sided or you may just become another statistic.

Background screening companies can help you with all of the background screening services you need, including pre-employment background checks for people you hire to help with home improvement projects, child care, home health care, or any other purpose.

SECRETS TO SAFETY

After two consecutive years of increases, the estimated number of violent crimes in the nation decreased 0.2 percent in 2017 when compared with 2016 data, according to FBI figures released today. Property crimes dropped 3.0 percent, marking the 15th consecutive year the collective estimates for these offenses declined.

The 2017 statistics show the estimated rate of violent crime was 382.9 offenses per 100,000 inhabitants, and the estimated rate of property crime was 2,362.2 offenses per 100,000 inhabitants. The violent crime rate fell 0.9 percent when compared with the 2016 rate; the property crime rate declined 3.6 percent.

These and additional data are presented in the 2017 edition of the FBI's annual report Crime in the United States. This publication is a statistical compilation of offense, arrest, and police employee data reported by law enforcement agencies voluntarily participating in the FBI's Uniform Crime Reporting (UCR) Program.

The UCR Program collects information on crimes reported by law enforcement agencies regarding the violent crimes of murder and nonnegligent manslaughter, rape, robbery, and aggravated assault as well as the property crimes of burglary, larceny-theft, motor vehicle theft, and arson. (The FBI classifies arson as a property crime, but it does not estimate arson data because of variations in the level of participation by the reporting agencies. Consequently, arson data is not included in the property crime estimate.) The program also collects arrest data for the offenses listed above plus 20 offenses that include all other crimes except traffic violations.

In 2013, the FBI's UCR Program initiated the collection of rape data under a revised definition within the Summary Reporting System. The term "forcible" was removed from the offense name, and the definition was changed to "penetration, no matter how slight, of the vagina or anus with any body part or object, or oral penetration by a sex organ of another person, without the consent of the victim." In 2016, the FBI Director approved the recommendation to discontinue the reporting of rape data using the UCR legacy definition beginning in 2017.

Of the 18,547 cities, counties, universities and colleges, state tribal, and federal agencies eligible to participate in the UCR Program, 16,655 agencies submitted data in 2017. A high-level summary of the statistics submitted, as well as estimates for those agencies that did not report.

In 2017, there were an estimated 1,247,321 violent crimes. The estimated number of robbery offenses decreased by 4.0 percent, and the estimated number of murder and nonnegligent manslaughter offenses decreased 0.7 percent when compared with estimates from 2016. The estimated volume of aggravated assault and rape (revised definition) offenses increased 1.0 percent and 2.5 percent, respectively.

- ➢ Nationwide, there were an estimated 7,694,086 property crimes. The estimated numbers for two of the three property crimes showed declines when compared with the previous year's estimates. Burglaries dropped 7.6 percent, larceny-thefts decreased 2.2 percent, but motor vehicle thefts rose 0.8 percent.

- ➢ Collectively, victims of property crimes (excluding arson) suffered losses estimated at $15.3 billion in 2017.

- ➢ The FBI estimated law enforcement agencies nationwide made 10.6 million arrests, (excluding those for traffic violations) in 2017.

- ➢ The arrest rate for violent crime was 160.7 per 100,000 inhabitants; the arrest rate for property crime was 388.7 per 100,000 inhabitants.

- ➢ By violent crime offense, the arrest rate for murder and nonnegligent manslaughter was 3.8 per 100,000 inhabitants; rape (aggregate total using the revised and legacy definition), 7.2;

robbery, 29.3; and aggravated assault, 120.4 per 100,000 inhabitants.

➢ Of the property crime offenses, the arrest rate for burglary was 61.7 per 100,000 inhabitants; larceny-theft, 296.0; and motor vehicle theft, 28.2. The arrest rate for arson was 2.8 per 100,000 inhabitants.

➢ In 2017, 13,128 law enforcement agencies reported their staffing levels to the FBI. These agencies reported that, as of October 31, 2017, they collectively employed 670,279 sworn officers and 286,662 civilians—a rate of 3.4 employees per 1,000 inhabitants.

The FBI launched the Crime Data Explorer (CDE) on June 30, 2017, in response to the need for law enforcement, the media, academia, and the American public to easily search for and find data from the UCR system. The CDE is a web-based, interactive environment where users can query, view, and download crime data. The CDE significantly changes the way UCR data is consumed and provides more specific and timely information. The 2017 crime data is now available in the CDE.

Caution Against Ranking: Each year when Crime in the United States is published, some entities use the figures

SECRETS TO SAFETY

to compile rankings of cities and counties. These rough rankings provide no insight into the numerous variables that mold crime in a particular town, city, county, state, tribal area, or region. Consequently, they lead to simplistic and/or incomplete analyses that often create misleading perceptions adversely affecting communities and their residents. Valid assessments are possible only with careful study and analysis of the range of unique conditions affecting each local law enforcement jurisdiction. The data user is, therefore, cautioned against comparing crime data of individual reporting units from cities, metropolitan areas, states, or colleges or universities solely on the basis of their population coverage or student enrollment.

According to the latest FBI Uniform Crime Reporting Statistics, property crime rates - including burglary, larceny, and motor vehicle theft - have seen a significant decline in the last few years:

- The 2015 property crime rate was 14.4% less than the 2011 estimate and 25.7% less than the 2006 estimate.

- The rate of property crime as a whole decreased from 13.9 victimizations per 1,000 households in 2014 to 11.2 per 1,000 in 2015 - a 19% change.

- Burglary, specifically, dropped from 701 per 100,000 people to 542 per 100,000 people - a 22% change.

- In comparing 2015 vs. 2016, preliminary data shows a 3.4% decrease in burglary crimes, with larger cities reporting a greater decrease at 5.9% than their nonmetropolitan counterparts at 4%.

- Keep in mind that statistics do vary significantly by region, for example, the Northeast showed the greatest decrease at 5.9%.

SECRETS TO SAFETY

- If you want to know how where you live compares, you can find the most recent crime statistics for your area in the FBI Uniform Crime Reporting Statistics.

While today's burglary statistics show an overall decrease in burglary rates, thousands of homes (roughly 325,000) are still being broken into every year - often in plain view, during the day. In fact, property crimes in 2015 resulted in losses estimated at $14.3 billion.

There is one burglary every 13 seconds.

There are roughly 2.5 million burglaries a year, 66% of those being home break-ins.

Police solve only 13% of reported burglary cases due to lack of a witness or physical evidence.

325,000 out of every 2.5 million incidents are solved.

2017 CRIME CLOCK STATISTICS

A Violent Crime occurred every	24.6 seconds
One Murder every	30.5 minutes
One Rape every	3.9 minutes
One Robbery every	1.7 minutes
One Aggravated Assault every	39.0 seconds
A Property Crime occurred every	4.1 seconds
One Burglary every	22.6 seconds
One Larceny-theft every	5.7 seconds
One Motor Vehicle Theft every	40.9 seconds

WHEN DO BURGLARIES OCCUR?

• There are 1,495,790 burglaries during the day. Break-ins are 6% more likely to occur during the day between 6 am and 6 pm while people are at work or running errands.

• There are 1,324,090 burglaries during the night. The cover of night brings security for intruders but also means people are more likely to be home.

• Snow and cold are also a significant deterrent. The lowest amount of burglaries happens in the month of February.

• A report from the U.S. Department of Justice showed that from 2005 to 2018, on average, burglary rates were highest in the summer, with about 9% lower rates in spring, 6% lower in fall, and 11% lower in winter.

FBI BURGLARY STATISTICS

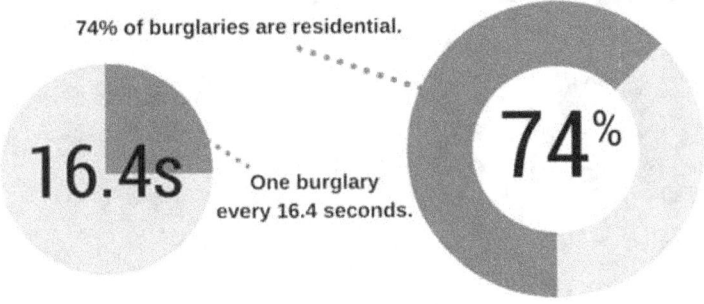

74% of burglaries are residential.

16.4s One burglary every 16.4 seconds.

74%

HOW DO THEY BREAK IN?

• Burglars are most attracted to homes that do not have a home security system, but only 17% of houses have a system in place.

• Homes without a security system are 300% more likely to be burglarized.

• 95% of all home invasions require some sort of forceful entry, be that breaking a window, picking a lock, or kicking in a door.

• The most common tools used for breaking in are pry bars, pliers, screwdrivers, and little hammers. All easily concealed and very common tools, making them harder to trace.

Burglaries
By the numbers

2.1 million	74.5%	$2,230
burglaries occurred in the U.S. in 2012	of all burglaries were residential	was the average property loss

WHO'S BREAKING IN?

A study on the habits and motivations of burglars conducted by the UNC Charlotte found:

• Burglars are most likely to be male and under 25 years old.

• 85% of break-ins are by amateurs and done out of desperation, which some might suggest makes them more dangerous.

• Most spend time considering factors like proximity to traffic and possible escape routes; 12% admitted to planning in advance while 41% said it was an impulsive decision.

• 83% admitted that they specifically look to see if there's an alarm; 60% would change their mind if there was one installed.

SECRETS TO SAFETY

CHAPTER 2

IS ANYONE HOME?

It's seems like the news reports are full of more and more stories of home invasions. There has always been a risk of burglary and most homeowner insurance policies cover the losses of a burglary. Burglars usually hit during the day when everyone is busy, and the house is empty. Burglars tend to choose a different house when they see an alarm system, strong locks and doors, and barred windows. Insurance companies will often offer a discount when homeowners have these things in place.

A burglar will usually run away if the homeowner should come home or be inside the house. Home Invaders usually hit home, at night or on weekends when someone is at home and security systems are deactivated. A home invasion is a situation where criminals will use force to get into a home with someone inside in order to rob or commit some other kind of crime. A home invasion is about gaining control of the home and the homeowner.

Some criminals understand convenience stores, banks and other major targets take steps to protect themselves and reduce their risks with alarms, surveillance and reduced cash on site. Many criminals know that homeowners may think their home is the last place on earth for a robbery or other crime. Families may feel so safe that they leave themselves as open and easy targets for the risk of a violent home invasion.

Home invaders might enter a home by kicking down a door or breaking a window. Their most likely point of attack is usually at the front door or garage. Home invaders like to impersonate delivery persons in order to have the homeowner open the door. It doesn't usually matter how home invaders enter, at some point they will use extreme force to take control of the home and family inside. At this point in a home invasion, a family's safety is at the most risk. Once the home invader takes control of the family often restraining them with duct tape, rope or handcuffs, home invaders usually search the families' home. Sometimes the family will be forced to, open safes, and provide PIN numbers and debit or credit cards.

Home invaders sometimes work in groups and depend on the fact they can overpower their targets when the perfect moment is there. In many cases, home invaders target residents who live in upscale neighborhoods. They may choose someone because of the car they drive or watch their shopping habit, the jewelry worn, or public event attended. Invaders may follow a person to their home.

A report on Victimization During Household Burglary found that:

• 27.6% of the time, a person is home while the burglary occurs; 26% of those people home are harmed. That means 7.2% of burglaries result in someone being injured.

• 65.1% of the attackers knew the victim and 27.5% were strangers.

- 60.5% of burglaries involved no weapon; 30.1% did involve a weapon; 9.3% of victims were unsure if a weapon was involved.

- Homes with an income of less than $7500 annually were most subject to being present while being burglarized, at 65.7 out of 1,000 homes. As you climb to higher and higher annual incomes, your chance of being present goes down.

- You are more likely to be burglarized if you rent than if you own your home.

- It seems as though burglars are less intimidated by people being present during an attack when they are either a single female, an American Indian or Alaskan Native, or if the house is occupied by anyone young, between the ages of 12-19 years old. Perhaps they feel less intimidated by groups of people.

- What is most likely to be taken? High-value items like electronics and personal items (including stamps, collections, recreational equipment, clothing, luggage, bikes, or animals). Also, anything that is small, easily pocketed, and can return a quick turn-around at a pawn shop.

SECRETS TO SAFETY

WHAT ARE MY PROTECTION OPTIONS?

Not surprisingly, burglars will typically avoid a house if it is too difficult or risky. The following are steps you can take to prevent home intrusion:

• Make your house less appealing by removing overgrown brush or other structures that can provide cover.

• Get metal doors or at least solid core wood on exterior entrances. Pair with a beefy deadbolt for good measure.

• To go the extra mile, install a heavy-duty strike plate with screws that go deep into the frame.

• Add a dowel or board into the track of sliding doors or windows. This prevents it from moving, even if it's unlocked.

• If you're keeping a window open, make sure it isn't more than 4 inches wide.

• Keep the entryway or porch locked, too. An open porch provides cover for those breaking into the main door.

- If someone you don't know knocks on the door loudly, make your presence known.

- If you choose to answer the door, do so while on the phone with a friend or pretend you're on the phone. This tells the potential burglar that someone will know if there's a break in.

- If you're sure a burglary is in progress, call 911 and shout loud statements like, "Honey - get the gun!" When they know you're aware and have self-defense measures in place they are much less likely to follow through.

- If you've just moved in, make sure you change the locks on all exterior doors to be safe.

- Get to know your neighbors. They're your first line of defense - you watch their house, they watch yours.

What are my protection options if I'm going on vacation?

- Stop your mail delivery or have a neighbor grab mail and packages until you return.

- Have your neighbor park their car in your driveway so it looks like someone is home.

SECRETS TO SAFETY

• Hook timers up to your televisions and lights. The same goes for outside lights - keep them on a timer or put them on motion-activated sensors.

• Hire a house sitter. Not only are they physically occupying your home, but they can also keep up on mail and trash for you and water your plants.

• If you have a large dog, that is a very common deterrent. However, dogs can also give away whether or not a person is home by their behavior. The bigger the dog, the less likely a thief is to attempt a break-in.

• Even if you don't have a dog, put a "Beware of Dog" sign up to suggest that you have a bully-breed dog that a robber should, in theory, be afraid of.

• Just the presence of an alarm system is enough to make a potential burglar reconsider. This is why security systems offer you a sign to put in your yard to warn the thieves.

• Leave a key and the alarm code with a trusted neighbor that is usually home when you're not so they can help if something happens.

• For particularly expensive or tempting items, carve your driver's license number and state somewhere inconspicuous so police can more easily match your stolen item.

- Create a shortlist of make, model, serial number and value of important items.

- Taking photos of your valuables. Keep a copy at home and give a copy to a trusted friend or family member, too.

- Check with your home insurance agent to make sure specific items are covered. You don't want to be caught in a loophole because of a technicality.

1) Most people's first excuse is that they can't protect themselves or can't learn self-protection. So let's find out what the true definition of "can't" is. According to the Webster's New Collegiate Dictionary printed in 1977, it states: can't, see cannot. "Cannot" is defined as "to be bound too; must." So where is the negative in the word?

2) The 2nd most common excuse is that I have NO TIME. So, let's look at the amount a time that we all have in an average day.

There are 24 hours in a day.

Subtract 8 hours for sleep.

That leaves you with 16 hours.

SECRETS TO SAFETY

Subtract another 8 hours for work/school.

That leaves you with 8 hours of discretionary time.

As you can see there are 8 hours left in a day and only, we/you can choose how to spend it.

3) The 3rd most common excuse is I CAN'T AFFORD IT. So, let us look at what does it really cost to learn self-protection. How much is your life worth to you? How much would it cost your spouse? How much would it cost for your children? This is the true value of a self-protection course because if you get sexually assaulted or raped you will NEVER be the same person you are today. If you get killed because you did not know how to protect yourself then your family and those that care about you will NEVER be able to replace YOU!

When it comes to protection, many people don't think they need a plan – at least, not right now. But things can change in a moment's notice. And, you want to be ready because chances are, there will be surprises ahead. Life is full of twists and turns and unexpected moments. You can't always see what's around the bend. But you can be ready for it.

3 CHAPTER

PLAY BY THE RULES

During my 20 years in law enforcement, I found that most homes I responded to for a burglary call had no idea the things they could have done to make their homes safer.

SECRETS TO SAFETY

Your analysis of your local problem should give you a better understanding of the factors contributing to it. Once you have analyzed your local problem and established a baseline for measuring effectiveness, you should consider possible responses to address the problem.

The following response strategies provide a foundation of ideas for addressing your particular problem. These strategies are drawn from a variety of research studies and police reports. Several of these strategies may apply to your community's problem.

It is critical that you tailor responses to local circumstances and that you can justify each response based on reliable analysis. In most cases, an effective strategy will involve implementing several different responses. Law enforcement responses alone are seldom effective in reducing or solving the problem.

Do not limit yourself to considering what police can do. Carefully consider whether others in your community share responsibility for the problem and can help police better respond to it.

The primary responsibility of responding, in some cases, may need to be shifted toward those who have the capacity to make more effective responses.

RULES OF SECURING YOUR HOME – OUTSIDE

1. Have a plan. The first line of defense is the exterior.

2. The second line of defense is the interior; secure valuables mark large possessions with your driver's license number. (T.V. Stereos, etc.).

You can help take the profits out of burglaries and thefts if you cooperate with your Police Department in this program. This program has been tested and proven not only in Denton but throughout the United States. By taking part in Operation Identification, you can greatly increase the risk that criminals must take if they steal your property.

How it works

Operation Identification operates in the following manner:

The Texas driver's license number of the head of the household is marked in some permanent manner on all valuable property, e.g. TX00649415. Do not mark property with a social security number. Marking should be in a place of prominence, which can be easily observed without dismantling the object. I suggest that an electric engraving pencil is used. As an added measure of protection, we encourage you to photograph items that cannot be easily marked. Also, record the serial numbers of your property even though you have marked it. Keep the serial number record with your other important papers.

If you purchase property that has another person's license number on it, merely add your own number to that property. Do not remove the other number. If you sell any of your valuable property, encourage the new owner to add his license number for proof of ownership.

3.   Your plan must cover your personal defense as well. Families need to develop a Home Invasion Plan; this includes having a "SAFE ROOM" in the house and a SAFE MEETING AREA" outside the house.

Develop a plan of action on what each member of the family will do in case the house is broken into when you are at home.

Years ago, most burglaries and rapes took place at NIGHT. Night time burglary and rapes still happen, but today we have a new breed of bolder criminal, most of whom are armed and many of whom like the THRILL of being in the house while you are sleeping. These guys don't value human life very much and are very dangerous.

PERIMETER SECURITY

•   The perimeter is the area surrounding your home or apartment. This is the first weakness for which the burglar/rapist looks. Can he approach you unnoticed?

•   Criminals avoid the spotlight. Porches, yards, and all entrances to your home and garage should be well lighted. Renters should make sure good lighting is available around the exterior of their building and in the parking lot because burglars like to hide in dark places where they cannot be seen.

•   Common area lighting around apartments should be on a timer or photocell to turn on at dusk and turn off at dawn.

•   Does your yard or sidewalk around your home/apt provide a VISUAL ZONE? If not:

o   Remove or cut back Trees, shrubs and bushes around windows and doors that may obscure the sides of your home from view. Thick, tall shrubbery provides cover for burglars and lets them work undetected.

•   Use Security mirrors on the corners of your house to see around your home.

Your ideal home security

Compact, single story homes are viewed as ideal.

Simple design – limited access points and no hidden spaces.

Boundaries should not be solid or too high – palisade fencing is ideal.

Fences or boundaries only necessary to keep children and animals inside property.

Signifiers of wealth generate risk.

INTERIOR SECURITY

• Make Your Home Look Occupied

• Leave lights on when you go out. A radio playing is also a good burglar deterrent. If you're going to be away for any length of time, connect some lamps to automatic timers so your lights turn on at dusk and off at bedtime.

• Don't allow daily deliveries to accumulate when you're gone. Cancel them in person or by phone or ask your neighbors to take in newspapers and advertising circulars. Never leave notes that can tip off burglars to your plans.

• Lower the sound of your telephone ringer and answering machine so they can't be heard outside.

• Have your lawn and walks taken care of. Dry uncut grass says you are away. Have snow shoveled from walks, steps, and drive.

• Get automatic timers. They help by turning lights on and off in different rooms at different times. If you do not have automatic timers, leave lights on in one or two interior rooms. They can make burglars think there is someone inside.

• When home, park your cars in the garage and close the garage door. This will make it more difficult for the

SECRETS TO SAFETY

thief to determine when you are home and when you are not. For example, if a thief realizes you always park your car in the driveway when you are home, they will wait to break in when the car is not in the driveway.

SECURE DOORS AND WINDOWS

The average burglar will spend no more than four to five minutes trying to break into a residence. A few simple security devices – nails, screws, padlocks, door, and window locks can slow burglars down and discourage them from entering your home.

DOORS

Exterior Doors - Statistics shows that almost 50% of all break-ins occur through either the front or rear door. Few burglars/rapist pick locks. Exterior doors, even those in your garage should be solid core wood or better still, steel construction and should be at least one inch (1") thick.

AVOID HAVING:

1. Glass doors or Glass too close to doors.

2. Hinges on the outside of doors.

As an extra security precaution, the door frame should also be steel. The door on the hinge side can have security studs or one-inch long bolts protruding from the hinged side of the door frame edge with a matching hole drilled in the frame so that when the door is closed, and the deadbolt locked the door frame and wall form one solid unit.

SECRETS TO SAFETY

INTERIOR DOORS

Any room in which you store valuables (your room, the children's room, etc.) should have solid core doors and have a double-keyed deadbolt lock so that you can secure this area when you are away from home. Again, hinges must be inside the room and security studs in the hinge side of the door will also help.

Peep Holes

If you do not have one, get one installed right away on all your exterior solid doors as well as your safe room. Be sure to buy a good one with a wide-angle lens and make sure that it has a glass lens, not the cheap plastic kind. Use it when you go answer the door.

Sliding Glass Doors (Note – I do not recommend the use of these doors.)

These doors have very flimsy locks that can be easily pried open. To prevent this, you can use a stick or locking anti-slide bar. A better alternative is a sliding door lock that mounts on the frame with long screws and sends a round bolt into the door frame when the key is turned. A solid lock prevents prying the lock or levering the door up from its frame. Check to make sure your sliding glass door has the sliding section installed on the inside.

• Pin-type locks or key locks work best in securing patio doors. Or, a steel rod can be inserted in the door channel. Additionally, put two or three screws in the overhead track to reduce the chance of lifting the door out of the track.

LOCKS

Entry doors come with a spring bolt lock standard. This type locks automatically when you close the door. The bolt is a wedge shape that slips into a striker plate on the door frame. One way to stop shimming is to have the door opening into the room, not to the outside. Also, an anti-shim strip can be added.

SECRETS TO SAFETY

DEAD-BOLTS

Every exterior / safe room entryway should be protected with a deadbolt lock. The deadbolt you buy should have a bolt long enough to go at least one- and one-half inches into the door support frame, not just the molding; I highly recommend that your deadbolt be the double-cylinder type. This type has a key slot on both sides. (In case of glass or a subject has an extra key). I recommend that you purchase the best available deadbolt locks. A good deadbolt lock will have the outside rim designed so it may rotate when a wrench is applied to it to prevent snapping the lock

Medico and Schlange make excellent mortise deadbolts. A top of the line brand is the Abloy lock. These are quite expensive and hard to find but they are worth the money and trouble. Cheap locks give cheap security.

The following are different types of locks available:

• Spring bolt locks can even be opened by inexperienced burglars. A credit card or other simple device is all that is needed to push back the lock bolt.

• Deadbolt locks should be installed on all exterior doors and doors from attached garages. There is a grading system that measures the security and durability of door locks. Locks that have undergone the testing required by the American National Standards

Institute (ANSI) are given a grade of 1, 2, or 3, with Grade 1 being the best. Therefore, it is recommended that homeowners' shop for a Grade 1 deadbolt lock.

A heavy-duty strike-plate should be installed using three-inch screws that penetrate the wall stud. Also, the door strike should be held in place by four or more screws. This will provide extra strength if a criminal tries to kick open the door.

Before you install new locks, it is a good idea to contact a reputable locksmith who can help you decide on the best lock for your situation and make sure you follow local regulations on locks.

SECRETS TO SAFETY

CHAIN LOCKS

Those little sliding chain locks are almost worthless (unless bolted into a steel door and frame). If a bad guy gets past your deadbolt any person over 175 1bs can easily kick it right off the frame.

Its only real use is to slow down an intruder. Make sure that the channel track that holds the chain is installed horizontally and not vertically. In the vertical position once the door is open you can easily reach in and slide the bolt up to release the chain. There are companies that make a slide bar version of this same lock, although this is a little better than a chain. Any lock of this type is only as good as the screws and hardware holding it to the frame.

Check the screws, if less than one inch (1") long replace those with one-inch long screws for the door lock assembly and at least two inches (2") in length for the door frame side. Drill slightly smaller holes than the size of the screws. Fill the holes with epoxy cement and install the screws. This will make the chain lock a bit more secure, but not much.

Never use the chain to open the door to a stranger or anyone you don't want to enter; thinking it will keep him out. IT WON'T!

KEYS

• Don't leave spare keys on hooks or nails. Hide them in a safe place. To avoid having so many keys call your locksmith, he can key most of your doors, window locks so that they have the same key.

• Do not leave a key under a doormat, flowerpot, or on a window ledge. Burglars look there first, it's too easy for someone to observe you taking it or putting it back.

• Don't give your key to anyone but your immediate family. An angry ex-friend or acquaintance of your son or daughter can have a duplicate key made for just a few dollars. Also, never leave an ignition key in your car, and never put a house key on your ignition key ring.

• If a key is lost and cannot be found in 24 hrs. as a precaution, you should change all the locks that key fits. If your child loses the key have them pay for the changing of the locks out of their own earnings.

• Secure windows with any of a variety of key locks available.

• Keep garage doors closed and locked. A locked garage door helps protect valuable property stored in your garage and prevents access to the interior of your residence.

SECRETS TO SAFETY

• Always lock your doors and windows when you leave the house. Past studies have indicated that most burglars enter through unlocked doors or windows.

• Verify the door locks have been changed before you move into your new home.

• Use a peephole to identify visitors before opening your door. If your building has an intercom-buzzer system, know who's calling before unlocking the lobby door.

WINDOWS

Sliding glass windows can be secured just like the sliding door with a locking device. Windows should be locked with a key-type lock.

I do not recommend the THUMB SCREW-TYPE sliding window locks. To be effective they have to be screwed down with pliers so that hand pressure cannot release them. This can be a hazard in a fire or emergency evacuation situation.

The best windows are those with small panes and a metal frame. Check to see if your window panes are set in with cheap putty. If so, you can secure the panes to the frame with super glue or ask a builder to replace the putty with a non-drying stronger adhesive.

BURGLAR BARS

If you have or will be installing such bars, make sure they have a quick release catch that is not accessible from the outside but that you can easily reach from inside in case of fire. Note: I'm not a strong advocate of these bars because of the dangers they pose in the event of a fire. If you chose to use them check with your local fire department for the best safety features and inspect them on a regular basis.

SECRETS TO SAFETY

WINDOW SHADES

Keep them closed at night and when you are not home.

GARAGE DOORS

If you have an attached garage you need a solid core door and deadbolt for the door going from the garage into the house.

The garage door itself should be able to be secured from within with a strong padlock. The door should not have a window that allows someone to look in and see if the garage is empty.

If you have an automatic opener, make sure that it puts the door all the way down when you enter. Some of the cheaper models are sensitive to power surges. Some professionals also have a little device like a television control box which plays random signals.

They drive down a street pushing the buttons and see whose door goes up. If you keep finding your door open, call the installer or door company and have it checked.

SECURITY ALARM SYSTEMS

It is debated whether having an alarm system decreases the chances of a burglary. In theory, if a burglar is aware a house has a system, he or she might move on to another home. Even if the alarm system does not keep a burglar from breaking in, the burglar tends to stay a shorter amount of time. This may decrease the number of items stolen and the extent of damage done.

Some of the basic elements of a standard home security system include:

- Control Panel

- Siren

- Door and window contacts

- A central monitoring system station (if you have a monitored alarm system)

- Keypad

- Inside motion detector

Protect keypad codes for gates, garage doors, and security systems by changing them often. Know who has keys and codes to your home.

SECRETS TO SAFETY

WHAT YOU SHOULD REALLY KNOW ABOUT ELECTRONIC ALARMS

The fact is that burglars will often case a home that looks like it may contain a lot of what they want to steal, even if it has an alarm.

A professional may come by, set off the alarm and go across the street to wait. He wants to see how long it takes the police to respond.

Points to Remember:

1. A thief may set off your alarm 2 – 3 times a month before he hits your home.

2. A thief does this to see police response time and establish a FALSE ALARM record.

TWO BASIC TYPES OF ALARMS

1.   Noise alert alarm - is connected to doors and windows. When tripped the alarm sets off sirens, bells, and/or turns on lights. (Least expensive)

2. Silent/authorities alert alarms - set off a signal at a central switching station. An operator checks the alarm and then calls the proper authorities.

Remember, most of these types transmit their signal over the phone line and if the phone is down or the wire is cut, your alarm may not work. Check phone lines to see if they are easily reached from the outside, if so have them secured (underground or encased in steel).

One important tip very few alarm companies call the police directly; some are even out of state, so check to see where the operations are stationed.

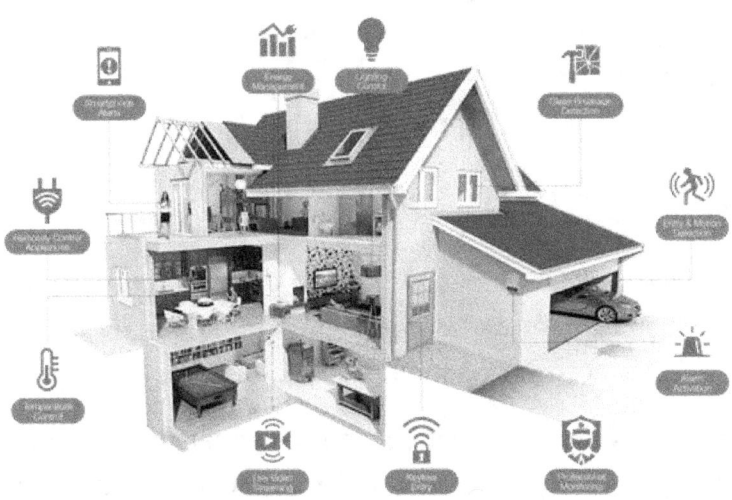

SECRETS TO SAFETY

NEIGHBORHOOD WATCH

Burglaries/Attacks can take place in broad daylight. Some crooks are so bold as to rent a truck, dress in coveralls and show up at your house after you go to work. They bypass the alarms, jimmy the door open and start loading your stuff.

Be a nosey neighbor. If you see such a truck/van parked at a neighbor's house do not go over to investigate. Call the neighbor on the phone. If you get no answer, call the police and tell them you think a burglary is in progress. Give a brief description of the VEHICLE, LICENSE PLATE NUMBER AND DESCRIPTION OF SUSPECT(S).

BE A "GOOD NEIGHBOR"

• Organize a "get-together" on common property of your apartment or in the neighborhood you live in so neighbors can get to know one another.

• Organize a Neighborhood or Apartment Watch program. Be on the lookout for suspicious activity and report it to the police.

• Arrange for local police to complete an apartment security survey.

- Alert the management of your apartment facility if you notice burned-out light bulbs, dark corridors, or broken locks on mailboxes and doors.

- If you hear an alarm going off, do not hesitate to call 911 for the police. It is better to be safe than sorry.

DOGS AS ALARMS

Bad guys don't like dogs because they make noise, attract attention and sometimes bite. Amateurs are often frightened away from a home if they see or hear a dog barking inside. In the house, a dog can pose more of a threat than one in the back yard.

Professionals do not fear dogs much and have many ways of neutralizing them with:

1. Chemical sprays

2. Poisoned or drugged laced meat

SECRETS TO SAFETY

HOME SAFETY RULES

IF YOU ARE AT HOME WHEN THE ALARM GOES OFF

RULE # 1

If he is in the same room, lie still and pretend to be asleep. DO NOT JUMP UP AND CONFRONT HIM

RULE # 2

If he is in another room, get to your safe room or get out of the house!

RULE # 3

Have a device by your bed that you can turn on all the lights in the house with a touch/turn of a button.

RULE # 4

REHEARSE YOUR ESCAPE! Look all through your home, what is the best escape route from each room in the house? If you have a two-story home or an upstairs apartment, can you go out the window with a cheap chain-type fire ladder?

Develop a safety plan with all members of your family. Have a plan of action in the event of a break in. Make sure everyone in the family knows what to do. Role play and practice going to the safe room and have a designated meeting spot outside of the home. Like the prairie dog have an "alarm call" (word, sound, whistle, etc.), so that when everyone hears it, they go to the safe room, use a different one for everyone to go to the designated meeting spot outside. Have an "all clear" (word, sound, whistle, etc.) when the danger has passed so everyone knows it is ok to come out of the safe room or come back inside. MAKE SURE SMALL CHILDREN UNDERSTAND THEY ARE NOT TO LEAVE A SAFE AREA UNLESS THEY HAVE HEARD THE "ALL CLEAR"!

HOME ANATOMY OF A BURGLARY

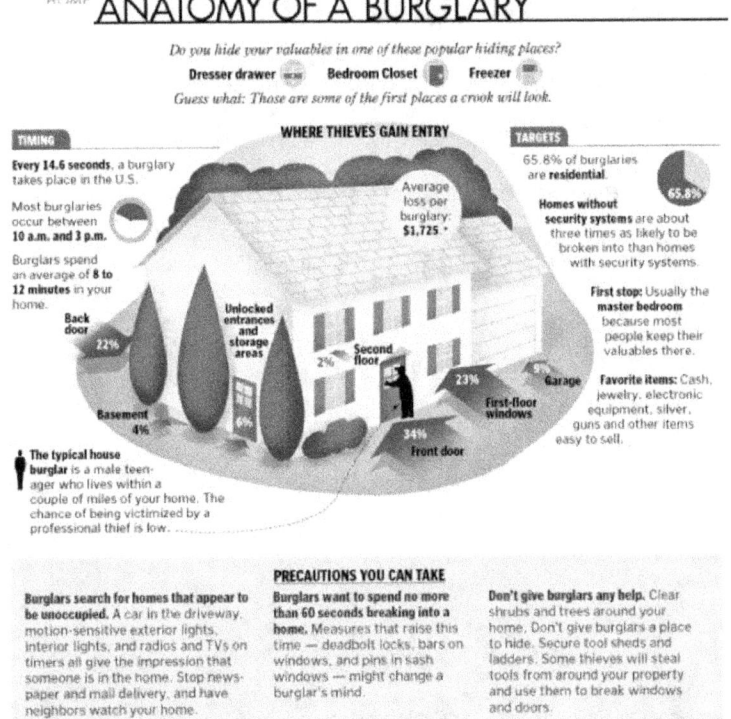

Do you hide your valuables in one of these popular hiding places?

Dresser drawer   **Bedroom Closet**   **Freezer**

Guess what: Those are some of the first places a crook will look.

TIMING

Every 14.6 seconds, a burglary takes place in the U.S.

Most burglaries occur between **10 a.m. and 3 p.m.**

Burglars spend an average of **8 to 12 minutes** in your home.

Back door 22%

Basement 4%

The typical house burglar is a male teen-ager who lives within a couple of miles of your home. The chance of being victimized by a professional thief is low.

WHERE THIEVES GAIN ENTRY

Average loss per burglary: **$1,725.**

Unlocked entrances and storage areas

Second floor 2%

First-floor windows 23%

Garage

Front door 34%

TARGETS

65.8% of burglaries are **residential.** 65.8%

Homes without security systems are about three times as likely to be broken into than homes with security systems.

First stop: Usually the **master bedroom** because most people keep their valuables there.

Favorite items: Cash, jewelry, electronic equipment, silver, guns and other items easy to sell.

PRECAUTIONS YOU CAN TAKE

Burglars search for homes that appear to be unoccupied. A car in the driveway, motion-sensitive exterior lights, interior lights, and radios and TVs on timers all give the impression that someone is in the home. Stop newspaper and mail delivery, and have neighbors watch your home.

Burglars want to spend no more than 60 seconds breaking into a home. Measures that raise this time — deadbolt locks, bars on windows, and pins in sash windows — might change a burglar's mind.

Don't give burglars any help. Clear shrubs and trees around your home. Don't give burglars a place to hide. Secure tool sheds and ladders. Some thieves will steal tools from around your property and use them to break windows and doors.

HAVE A SAFE ROOM

SECRETS TO SAFETY

A SAFE ROOM is an area to which you can retreat and wait for the police to arrive when it is not practical to go out of the house. No matter how large or small your safe room is it should contain the following things:

1.   A solid core door and two (2) deadbolt locks. One of the locks is installed on the hinge side of the door, the other on the door knob side.

2.   A cordless and cellular phone.

3.   An electric plug for the phone to charge

4.   Flashlight with batteries.

5.   The personal weapon of your choice (stun gun, pepper mace, etc.)

6.   A Peephole in the door.

7.   A bottle of fresh water and snacks.

WHEN THE POLICE DO COME

RULE # 1   NEVER meet the officer at the door or yard with a firearm in your hands.

RULE # 2   Be polite

RULE # 3   Have suspect information

SECRETS TO SAFETY

HOME SECURITY CHECKLIST

OUTSIDE

❏ Is the visual zone around the building at least ten (10) feet?

❏ Are shrubs trimmed back for good vision?

❏ Does outdoor lighting illuminate the entire building on all sides?

❏ Are all security lights high enough to avoid being reached from the ground?

❏ Are all security lights covered with wire to prevent breakage?

❏ If there is a wood fence are the rungs facing into the yard?

❏ Do all windows have heavy drapes or shades to prevent viewing in at night?

❏ Garage doors of steel or solid core with no windows.

HOME SECURITY CHECKLIST

INSIDE

❑ All exterior doors and safe room door are made of solid core wood or steel construction.

❑ All exterior doors especially those with glass panels have double deadbolt lock.

❑ All solid exterior doors and safe room door have wide angle peephole.

❑ Windows have key locks or bar/grating over windows.

❑ Windows are multi-paned with steel, not wood frame.

❑ Security alarm system is installed.

❑ Wall, floor or hidden safe for valuables.

❑ Cellular phone or second phone line by bed or near safe room door.

❑ Escape ladder under bed if second-story home or apartment.

❑ A closet or area converted to a safe room.

SECRETS TO SAFETY

❑ A dog that barks as anyone approaches your home. If you do not have a dog, a recording of a dog barking will suffice.

❑ A central place to leave all keys so they are readily available.

❑ A spare set of keys on one ring in the safe room.

SPECIAL NOTE

If you don't have these vital safety features, then immediately do everything to remedy the situation.

Other precautions you should take

- Do not keep valuable jewelry at home. Keep it, along with other small valuables and important documents, in a safe deposit box. If you choose not to use a safe deposit box, place items of high value in areas of low risk, such as an unusual hiding place.

- Keep a detailed inventory of all your personal possessions and include the date of purchase, original value, and serial numbers. Save the sales receipts for your more valuable belongings and keep them with your inventory list. It's also a good idea to photograph your belongings, especially valuable ones like antiques.

- Never leave valuables inside cars overnight.

SECRETS TO SAFETY

CHAPTER 4

THE REAL TRUTH ABOUT RAPE

When a woman has a close personal relationship with the man who rapes her, she (and others) may be confused about whether the attack was really a rape.

The law, however, is clear on the subject of marital rape. Texas has been a leader among the states in asserting that the marriage contract does not erase a wife's right to say no to her husband. A woman in this state who is raped by her husband has the same rights as any other victim of rape, and she can receive the same protection under the Family Abuse Prevention Act as a woman who is beaten by her husband.

Similarly, what some call "date rape" is in fact the crime of rape. The term "date rape'" should not be used, as it is never appropriate to define a crime in the context in which it sometimes happens. For example, you would never hear, "it was a walk-in-the-park mugging".

Sexual assaults and rapes are planned; they are not the results of unpredictable bursts of passion. The plan often is subtle and intricate, involving covert threats and manipulative actions. For example, earlier in the evening, the sexual offender might have demonstrated his strength in a playful wrestling match, or he may have shown her his gun collection or happened to mention violent acts he had committed in the past. The purpose is to plant the seeds of fear that will undermine her defenses when he attacks her.

Rapists will often rationalize, "It was a date, and she knew what to expect" (as if all dates are supposed to involve rape); or, "She shouldn't have drunk so much if she didn't want to do it" (since when is trusting someone an invitation to rape?); or, "She didn't fight or scream" (as if being immobilized by fear or shock should be construed as consent).

Women who have been raped by their husbands or acquaintances experience many of the same fears and feelings as the victim of any sexual assault. They suffer from guilt ("Was it something I said? Or did?"), from fear ("What if it happens again?"), and from loss of trust ("How could he do this to me?").

The victim needs to know that the attack was planned and nothing she did or did not do caused his sexually assaultive behavior. She needs to hear that he is a criminal and she is not an accessory to the crime but rather a victim. She needs to understand that her reactions during the assault—whether she chose nonresistance or screaming or some other tactic—were what she needed to do to survive. Only her instincts could tell her his potential for violence at that time, and she was correct to trust her instincts. Whether or not she chooses to prosecute, we encourage her to contact someone trained to work with sexual assault victims so that her healing process may begin as quickly as possible.

TEST QUESTIONS: TRUE OR FALSE

1. Rape is forced sexual relations against a person will.

2. Rape is the most frequently committed violent crime in the United States.

3. Over 50% of all rape occurs between people who have met before.

4. The majority of reported rapists are between 15 and 24 yrs. of age.

5. Most rapes occur between people of the same race and similar social position.

6. An estimated 50% of all rapes are never reported to the police.

7. Rape takes place during daytime hours and often in the victim's home.

SECRETS TO SAFETY

8. Studies show that rapists plan ahead and choose women who seem likely to be "victims".

9. Rapists interviewed say they have poor social relations with women.

10. Sexual gratification is not the motivating factor in rape.

11. Rape is an expression of hostility, aggression, and dominance.

12. All victims of rape, regardless of their previous sexual experience, report rape as a violent and dangerous attack upon them that deeply affects their lives.

HOW DID YOU DO? Answers to quiz: #4 & #6 are False. All the rest are True!

SOME MYTHS AND FACTS ABOUT RAPE

There are many myths about rape, sexual assault, domestic violence, and date rape. This book is to dispel those myths by educating you with the facts. Then give you some basic self-defense techniques that if practiced you should be able to handle yourself should you be physically or mentally confronted.

Myth: The primary motive for rape is sexual.

Fact: Rape cannot happen to a decent woman/man. Only women who act or dress provocatively or who are sexually promiscuous get raped. They asked for it!

Myth: The primary motive for rape is aggression.

Fact: Most rapists have available sexual relationships. Rape is aggression against women/men. Motivated by the need to abuse, humiliate and degrade them. It is a crime of violence committed by men/women incapable of handling their anger, frustration and/or helplessness without brutalizing and hurting others.
Most rape victims have good reputations in their communities. Becoming a victim is not related to a person's dress, provocative manner or sexual habits. Full clothed grandmothers and babies in diapers have

75

been victims of rape. Any person regardless of sex, age, appearance or social status can be raped and nobody deserves to be violated, abused and subjected to the emotional damaging crime.

Myth: Women actually enjoy rape.

Fact: Women enjoy consensual relationships, but rape is not sexual and definitely not consensual. Attacks, intimidation, injury, abuse, humiliation, threats and degradation are not enjoyable.

Myth: A woman who really tries can prevent rape.

Fact: Anyone can be immobilized by fear and the threat of death or violence. A person's size and strength has little bearing on their ability to prevent rape. Psychological preparedness can help to overcome the paralyzing effects of terror; proper safety precautions can reduce vulnerability.

Myth: Rapists are impulsive, motivated by uncontrollable desires on the spur of the moment. It's usually a one-time thing.

Fact: Most rapes are planned, and the victim is chosen on the basis of vulnerability. Rapists are often repeating offenders. They've raped before and will do it again.

Myth: Women are raped by strange men in dark alleys.

Fact: While about half of therapists are strangers of the victim, social rape (where the victim knows the rapists) is still indisputably rape. Whenever a person is forced, against their will, to submit to unwanted sexual relations, it is rape—and not a successful seduction by a lover, friend, acquaintance, neighbor or stranger.

PERSONAL SAFETY BEGINS WITH AWARENESS!!!

The vulnerability may result from age, handicaps, intoxication, living alone, walking or traveling alone, darkness, being stranded or from trusting strangers.

DON'T TAKE CHANCES!!!

SECRETS TO SAFETY

FACTS ABOUT SEXUAL ASSAULT

Definition of "Sexual Assault"; Penal Code 22.011 (a)(1)(A)(B)(C)

a)   a person commits an offense if:

1)   the person Intentionally or knowingly:

A.   Causes the penetration of the anus or sexual organ of another person by any means, without that person's consent;

B.   Causes the penetration of the mouth of another person by the sexual organ of the actor, without that person's consent; or

C.   Causes the sexual organ of another person, without that person's consent, to contact or penetrate the mouth, anus, or sexual organ of another person, including the actor.

THREE METHODS OF GAINING SEXUAL ACCESS TO A PERSON

A)   CONSENT: Both parties freely participate as a result of mutual interest and negotiation.

B)   PRESSURE: An unwilling person is coerced or intimidated into sexual activity by a person in a position of power or dominance. Refusal may have economic, vocational, or social consequences. Penal Code 22.011(2)(b)(8).

C)   FORCE: Risk bodily harm, injury, or death if the victim refuses to participate in sexual activity, or the inability to physically escape   Penal Code 22.011(2)(b)(2).

SECRETS TO SAFETY

SEXUAL ASSAULT STATISTICS

A) 1 in 3 women are sexually assaulted. That's 1.3 per minute, 78 per hour, 1,871 per day and 683,000 per year.

B) For any female who is age 14 or older, the odds of becoming a sexual assault victim in her lifetime are 1 in 3

C) It is estimated that 90% of sexual assaults are NOT reported to police.

D) The two most common articles of clothing worn by sexual assault victims at the time of the assault are nightgowns and blue jeans.

E) Of all the sexual assault cases reported in the U.S., the location of the crime is:

a. 50% of the time in the victim's home.
b. 25% of the time in a friend's home;
c. 25% of the time in other locations.

LAWS PERTAINING TO SEXUAL ASSAULT

Two Primary Texas Penal Code Statutes
A) Section 22.011-Sexual Assault
B) Section 22.021 -Aggravated Sexual Assault

OFFENSE OF "Sexual Assault"
Elements required to commit an offense:

A) ADULTS - A person Intentionally or knowingly:

1. Causes the penetration of the anus or sexual organ of another person by any means, without that person's consent;

2. Causes the penetration of the mouth of another person by the sexual organ of the actor, without that person's consent; or

3. Causes the sexual organ of another person, without that person's consent, to contact or penetrate the mouth, anus, or sexual organ of another person, including the actor.

B) CHILDREN — Regardless of whether the person knows the age of the child at the time of the offense, the person Intentionally or knowingly:

1. causes the penetration of the anus or sexual organ of a child by any means;

2. causes the penetration of the mouth of a child by the sexual organ of the actor;

3. causes the sexual organ of a child to contact or penetrate the mouth, anus, or sexual organ of another person, including the actor;

4. causes the anus of a child to contact the mouth, anus, or sexual organ of another person, including the actor; or

5. causes the mouth of a child to contact the anus or sexual organ of another person, including the actor.

C) ADULTS, "WITHOUT CONSENT" - A sexual assault under Subsection (a)(1) is without the consent of the other person if:

1. Physical threat or violence is used to compel the victim to submit;

2. Threat of force or violence is used to compel the victim to submit, and the victim believes the actor has the ability to carry out the threat;

3. A non-consenting person is incapacitated or is physically unable to resist;

4. The actor knows that as a result of mental disease or effect, victim is incapable of understanding the nature of the act or resisting it;

5. The victim has not consented, and the actor knows the victim is unaware the sexual assault is occurring;

6. The actor has impaired the victim by administering any substance without the victim's knowledge; or

7. Threat of force or violence against any person is used to compel the victim to submit, and the victim believes the actor has the ability to carry out the threat.

D) "Child" is defined by this section as: A person younger than 17 years of age who is not married to the actor.

E) An offense under this Section is a 2nd degree FELONY (2-20 years in state prison and a potential maximum fine of $10,000 or both.)

F) Prosecution of a Spouse under this Section requires: A showing of bodily injury or threat of bodily injury.

G) Regarding children, it is a defense to prosecution if:
1. The child at the time of the offense was 14 years of age or older,
2. The conduct consisted of medical care for the child.

H) It is an affirmative defense to prosecution for sexual assault of a child if the actor was not more than 2 years older than the victim.

("Affirmative defense to prosecution" as defined in Sec. 2.04, TPC, means the issue of existence of an affirmative defense is not presented to the jury unless evidence supporting the defense is admitted. In such case, the court shall instruct the jury that the defendant must prove the affirmative defense by a "preponderance of evidence" or, in other words, the evidence supporting the defense must be more credible and outweigh the evidence against the defense. In simpler terms, the defendant must raise the issue of the defense and it's up to the defendant to prove it.)
OFFENSE OF "AGGRAVATED SEXUAL ASSAULT"

Elements required to commit an offense:

A) ADULTS – The same elements as listed above for "Sexual Assault" are present and the perpetrator:

1. Causes serious bodily injury or attempts to cause death of the victim or another person in the course of the same criminal episode;

2. By acts or words, places the victim in fear that death, serious bodily injury, or kidnapping will be imminently inflicted on any person;

3. By acts or words occurring in the presence of the victim, threatens to cause death, serious bodily injury, or kidnapping of any persons;

4. Uses or exhibits a deadly weapon in the course of the same criminal episode; or

B) CHILDREN – The same elements as listed above for "Sexual Assault" are present and the perpetrator:
The victim is younger than 14 years of age.

1. The "Sexual Assault" defense to prosecution of the child being 14 years of age and promiscuous does NOT apply here.

2. The "Sexual Assault" affirmative defense to prosecution that the actor was not more than two years older than the victim does NOT apply here.

3. An offense under this Section is a 1st degree FELONY (confinement in state prison for 5-99 years or for life, and a potential maximum fine of $10,000 or both).

A. INDECENT EXPOSURE – Sec. 21.08, TPC

1.   A person commits an offense if he/she knowingly exposes his/her anus or any part of the person's genitals with intent to arouse or gratify the sexual desire of any person and the actor is reckless about whether another is present who will be offended or alarmed by the act:

B.   An offense under this section is a Class B Misdemeanor.

A. INDECENCY WITH A CHILD – Sec. 21.11, TPC

1. A person commits an offense if, with a child younger than 17 years and not the actor's spouse, whether the child is of the same or opposite sex, the actor:

(a) engages in sexual contact with the child; or cause the child to engage in sexual contact;

(b) exposes his/her anus or any part of the person's genitals, knowing the child is present, with intent to arouse or gratify the sexual desire of any person.

2. It is a defense to prosecution under this section that the child was at the time of the alleged offense 14 years or older.

3. It's an affirmative defense to prosecution under this section that the actor:

a. was not more than three years older than the victim and of the opposite sex; and

b. did not use duress, force, or a threat against the victim at the time of the offense.

c. An offense under (a)(1), above is a 2nd Degree Felony and an offense under (2)(2), above is a 3rd Degree Felony.

B. PUBLIC LEWDNESS – Sec. 21.07, TPC

A person commits an offense if he/she knowingly engages in any of the following acts in a public place or, if not in a public place, is reckless about whether another is present who will be offended or alarmed by the act:

1. An act of sexual intercourse;
2. An act of deviate sexual intercourse;
3. An act of sexual contact;
4. An act involving contact between the person's mouth or genitals and the anus or genitals of an animal or fowl.

An offense under (a)(1), above, is a Second-Degree Felony and an offense under (2)(2), above, is a Third-Degree Felony.

EVIDENCE OF A VICTIM'S PREVIOUS SEXUAL CONDUCT, Rule 412 (RCE):

1) Opinion and Reputation evidence of alleged victim's past sexual behavior is NOT admissible;

2) Evidence of specific instances of alleged victim's past sexual behavior is NOT admissible unless certain conditions exist (see Rule in its entirety);

3) If a defendant proposes to introduce any documentary evidence to ask any questions concerning specific instances of the alleged victim's past sexual behavior, the defendant must:

a. Inform the court without the jury present of the desire to introduce such evidence; and

b. The court shall then conduct a private hearing (without the jury present) as to whether the evidence is admissible

SECRETS TO SAFETY

AIDS TESTING, Art. 21.31 CCP

A. A person indicted for an offense under Sec. 22.011, TPC (Sexual Assault) or 22.021, TPC (Aggravated Sexual Assault) shall, at the direction of the court, undergo a medical procedure to test to determine if the person as a sexually transmitted disease, or has acquired immune deficiency syndrome (AIDS) or human immunodeficiency virus (HIV) infection, antibodies to HIV, or infections with any other probable causative agent of AIDS.

B. The person performing the test shall make the test results known to the local health authority, and the local health authority shall be required to make notification of the test results to the alleged victim. Otherwise, the test results are confidential.

CORROBORATION OF VICTIM'S TESTIMONY, Art. 38.07 CCP

A. Corroboration of testimony is not required to support a conviction, if:

1. The victim informed any person, other than the defendant, of the alleged offense within 6 months after the date on which the offense is alleged to have occurred; or

2. The victim was 17 years of age or 14 years at the time of the alleged offense.

B. The judge shall instruct the jury that the time which elapsed between the alleged offense and the time it was reported shall be considered by the jury only for the purpose of assessing the weight to the victim's testimony.

COST OF SEXUAL ASSAULT MEDICAL EXAM, Art. 56.06 CCP

A. All cost of a medical exam for use in the investigation or prosecution of a sexual assault case shall be paid by the law enforcement agency that requests such exam of an alleged sexual assault victim.

B. This article does NOT require the law enforcement agency to pay any costs of treatment of alleged victim's injuries.

SECRETS TO SAFETY

COMMON MYTHS AND FACTS

A.   MYTH: Some women could never be raped. (Too old, ugly, fat, etc.)
FACT: All women (young, old, fat, slim, pretty, ugly) are potential victims of sexual assault.

B.   MYTH: Rape is only a crime against women.
FACT: Rape is a crime against women and men. Not only are men raped by other men, but men can also be raped by women.

C.   MYTH: Rape is a sexual act.
FACT: Rape is sexual aggression and violence. 87% of offenders brandish a weapon or threaten the victim with injury or death.

D.   MYTH: Rape is a crime committed by strangers.
FACT: Rape is most often committed by relatives, friends, neighbors, or acquaintances of the victim.

E.   MYTH: Most rapes occur at night in a public place.
FACT: Most rapes occur in the afternoon or evening in the victim's home (or place of employment). As a result, many victims suffer increased trauma since the violation occurred at a time and place, they believed were safe.

92

F.   MYTH: Women secretly want to be raped.

FACT: Women rarely fantasize about being raped, and if they do, it is in terms of aggressive sex. Women do not desire or want to be violently or brutally assaulted by a person not of their choosing any more than men do.

G.   MYTH: Most rapes are inter-racial.

FACT: Most rapes involve persons of the same race or culture.

H.   MYTH: Some ask to be raped by their dress or actions.

FACT: Most rapes are planned and based on the offenders' perception that a victim is an easy and vulnerable target.   No one "asks" or deserves to be victimized even if their behavior places them at high risk.

I. MYTH: You really can't rape a non-consenting adult female.

FACT: It is entirely possible to rape anyone. Fear of greater harm brought on by believable threats can produce submission, as an overwhelming force.

J.   MYTH: Victims often lie about being sexually assaulted.

SECRETS TO SAFETY

FACT: Victims rarely fabricate a story about being sexually assaulted. Although some cases are unfounded, all of the disadvantages of making a police report prevent most victims from reporting at all, and far outweigh the motivations of most people who would falsify a report. FBI statistics have shown the false reporting rate for sexual assault is about the same as for all felony crimes (4%). Victims do, however, leave out embarrassing or perceived incriminating details, or block important facts.

K. MYTH: There is nothing anyone can do to prevent rape.

FACT: There is no way to guarantee it can't happen. There are, however, a number of ways to reduce the risk of rape by increased awareness and personal safety precautions.

CLARIFYING MISCONCEPTIONS HELPS US UNDERSTAND WHY VICTIMS ARE AFRAID TO REPORT THE CRIME and prosecute the offender.

Not only does the victim face a generally unsympathetic public, but also in many jurisdictions' victims own personal credibility, worthiness, and lifestyle are placed on trial.

94

VICTIMS ARE JUST AS LIKELY TO BELIEVE THESE MISCONCEPTIONS as anyone else.

These distorted beliefs are often a significant contributing factor to a victim's defensive or hostile behavior and may result in the inability to recover from emotional trauma. Even with the best interviewing techniques. The victim may accuse the interviewer of not believing her or blaming her. Victims often believe the myths about sexual assault and may "externalize" their feelings on the interviewer.

SECRETS TO SAFETY

CHAPTER 5

SELF DEFENSE THAT WORK

Witnessing the dramatic escalation in violent crimes such as, muggings and sex crimes in the late 60's, Ed Parker Sr., the father of four daughters, felt a need for a realistic method of defense for the cornered woman— the woman who has no means of escape or foreknowledge of an attack. In 1968, he wrote a book specifically for women entitled, complete, with uncluttered black and white line drawings by Jim McQuade for ease of comprehension, women everywhere would be able to follow this step-by step practical guide. Natural weapons and proper blocks were incorporated directly into self-defense techniques and presented as interchangeable methods. All of the techniques, specifically designed by Ed, were tailored appropriately so that a woman could apply many of them without using a great deal of force. In this straightforward, to the point, printed work, Ed introduced the use of personal and/or household articles as weapons, such as, an umbrella, a broom, a lipstick or a comb. Still after 45 years these techniques prove to be a real aid to instructors giving practical, no nonsense self-defense courses to youth and women's groups throughout the world.

In his book Infinite Insights into Kenpo, Volume 1, Mental Stimulation, Delsby Publications, © 1982, Edmund K. Parker, SGM Ed Parker wrote that "daily actions, if analyzed, can be classified as latent, formidable, working, and effective natural weapons." SGM Ed Parker provided the following illustrations as examples:

SECRETS TO SAFETY

I-21a Just a simple step while walking...

I-21b could be exaggerated and converted into a knee kick.

I-22a We walk using the opposite foot and the opposite arm.

I-22b With power and extension, the same hand movement can be effectively used against an opponent's groin.

The general thinking is that muscle memory takes over in any given situation. The memory of common practical movement can be turned into life saving techniques in the right instances.

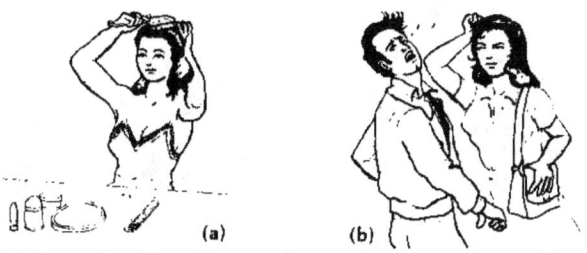

1-23a & b The action of brushing your hair can be converted to an elbow strike to an assailant's jaw.

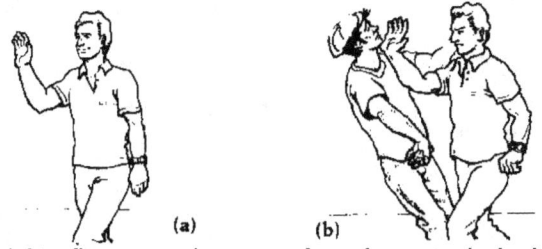

1-24a & b A friendly wave can be converted to a devastating heel palm strike to an opponent's jaw.

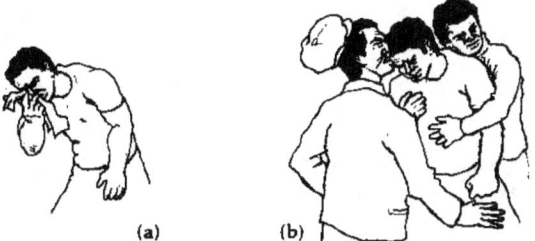

1-25a & b A simple sneeze can be converted to a rewarding head butt to an opponent's nose.

Practical movements like brushing one's hair, waving hello or even blowing one's nose can be a self defense measure that can easily be taken without thinking about the movement.

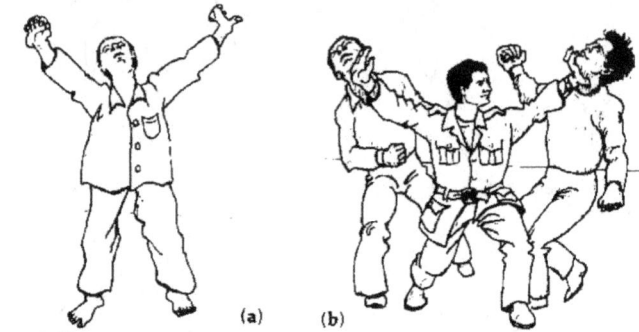

(a) (b)

I-26a & b The action of a good morning stretch can be simultaneously used against two assailants with victorious results.

(a) (b)

I-27a & b Side stepping water splashed from a passing car can be converted into an effective stomp on the foot of an opponent.

Stretching or a simple jump backwards can dismay an opponent.

In Ed Parker's book The Woman's Guide to Self-Defense, ©1968 by Iron Man Industries Alliance, Nebraska, Instruction by Ed Parker, illustrated by Jim McQuade. SGM Ed Parker illustrated the following:

**C — HOW TO COUNTER AN ATTACK WHILE LYING ON YOUR BACK
(VARIATION)**

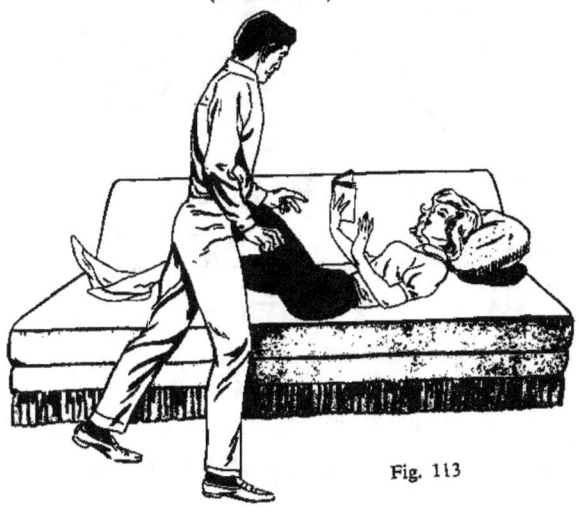

Fig. 113

Fig. 113. Opponent is approaching you while you are lying on your back on a couch.

Fig. 114. As opponent crouches to molest you, use your left hand to grab the clothing of your opponent's left shoulder, simultaneously delivering a right heel thrust to your opponent's chin.

Fig. 114

Fig. 115

115. Grab the clothing of your opponent's right shoulder with your right hand and pull in with your left arm as you push out with your right.

116. After forcing your opponent on his back, drop upon opponent as you force your right knee into his groin and your right elbow into his throat.

Fig. 116

**D — HOW TO COUNTER FROM
A KNEELING POSITION**

Fig. 117

Fig. 117. Opponent grabs your shoulder while you are kneeling to dust the furniture.

Fig. 118. Raise up on your left leg (keeping that knee bent) and deliver a rear scoop kick to the groin (using the back of your heel).

Fig. 118

SECRETS TO SAFETY

REAR CHOKE/ GRAB DEFENSES

As the attacker reaches around for a single arm choke. The defender should always be aware of their surroundings and be prepared for anything. By raising the hands up and between you and the choker, this eliminates the possibility of being choked out or passing out during an attack.

SECRETS TO SAFETY

Allowing an attacker to grab around the neck area can be lethal.

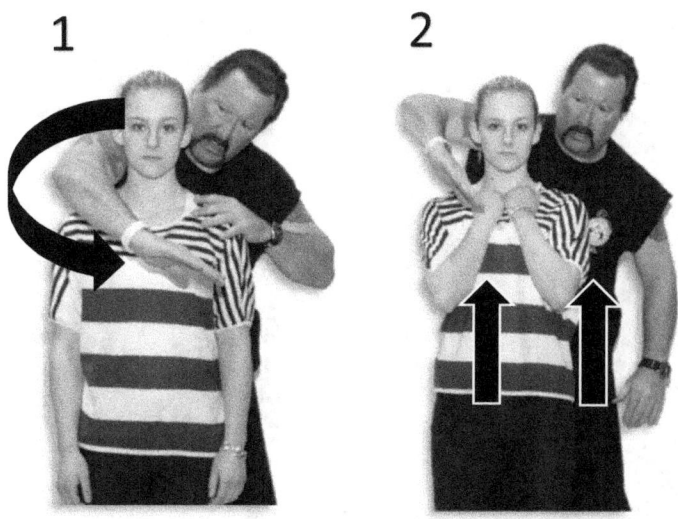

The defender raises both hands straight up to their chin. This can help prevent a choking situation where the defender cannot breathe.

1-4. Raising your hands to your chin and under the arms of the attacker during this type of attack prevents the attacker from choking.

SECRETS TO SAFETY

1-4. The attacker grabs around from behind attempting to hold / control the defender.

5

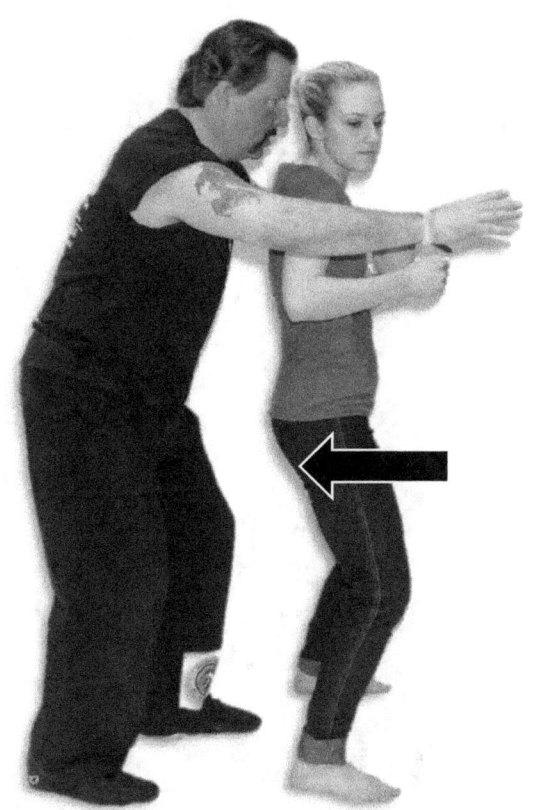

5. Defender uses the elbow to strike backwards in to the attacker's body. Ribcage, side of body, chest are all sensitive areas.

6

6. Defender smashes elbow in to the attacker's body.

7

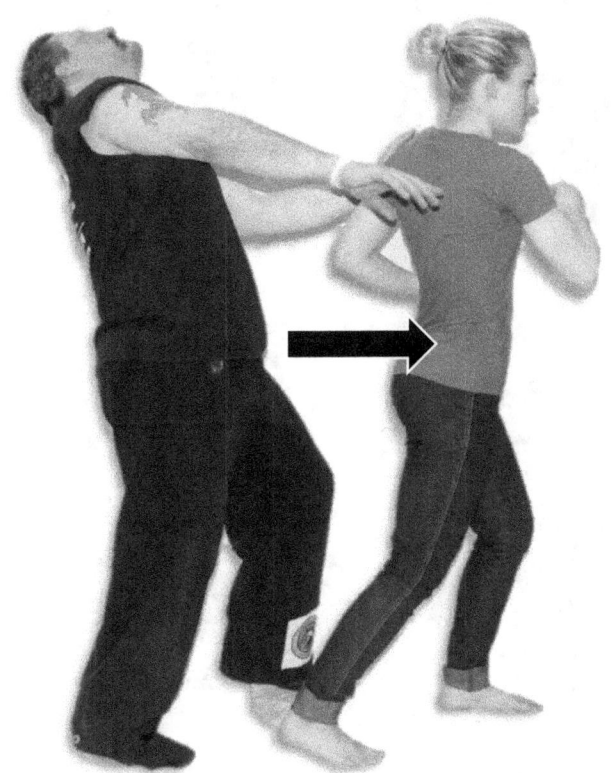

7. Once free defender should run away.

DO NOT STAY AND FIGHT. RUN AWAY

1-4. Attacker attempts to grab hold from behind.

5

5. Defender uses the elbow to strike vital areas of the attacker's body. Thrusting the elbow backwards toward the attacker's body.

6

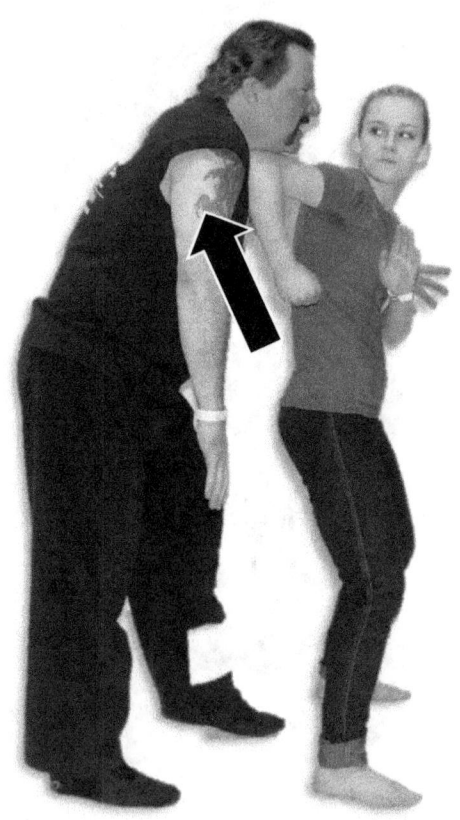

6. Defender strikes the elbow upward toward the jaw / face of attacker.

7

7. The defender strikes hard to the jaw / face of attacker.

8

8. Striking the Face / Jaw of attacker upwards can cause serious injury. The attacker can easily bite down on his tongue or inside the cheek. The strike may also move upwards toward the nose fracturing / breaking the nose bone / cartilage.

9

9. The defender runs away. Go directly to police or seek help in a public place when possible.

DO NOT STAY AND FIGHT RUN AWAY

SECRETS TO SAFETY

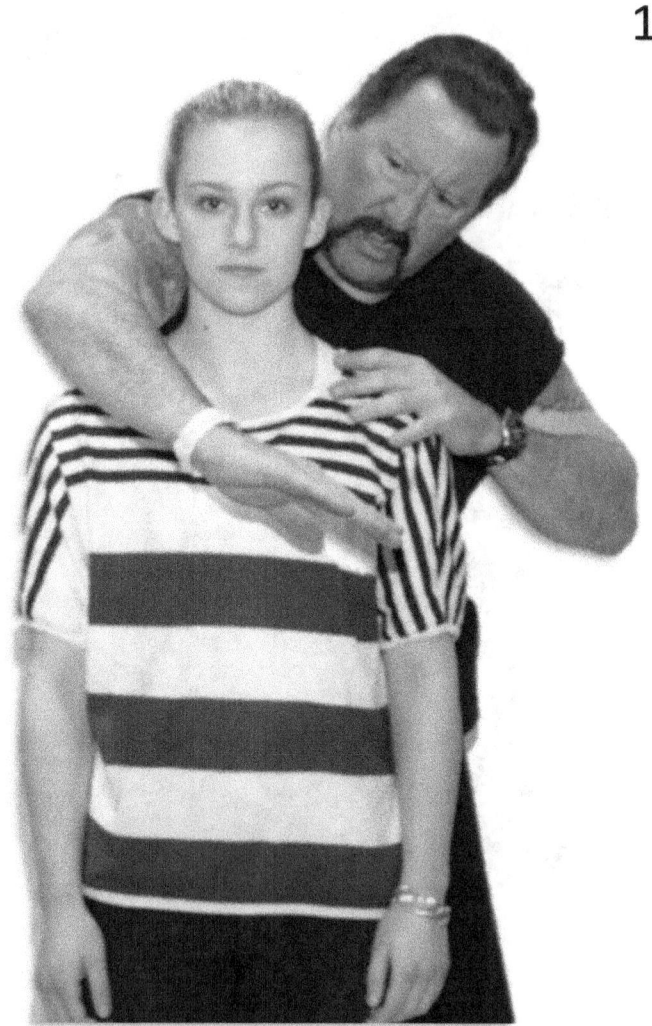

1. Attacker reaches around from behind to choke /
   hold defender.

2. As the attacker reaches around the neck, an alternative to raising your hands to neck level is by simply turning your head toward the inside of the attacker's arm. This is a good prevention as well from a choke assualt.

119

3

As the attacker reaches around, Defender grabs fingers / Fingertips of the attacker. (Close-Up) grabbing the fingers of the attacker firmly.

4

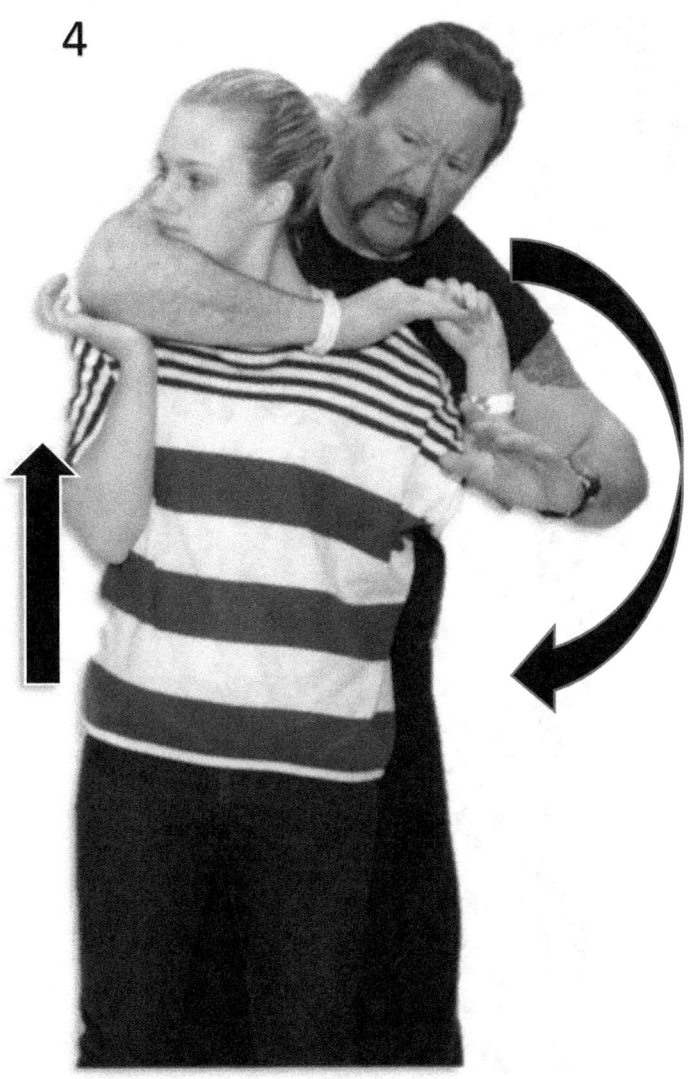

Pushing up on the outside of the elbow of the attacker and pulling fingertips outward and away from your body allows space to move out of the choke hold position.

5

5. Pushing up/ lifting on the outside of the elbow of the attacker and pulling fingertips outward away from your body allows space to move out of the choke hold position.

6

6. Pushing outward and away on the attacker's elbow while pulling back and down on the attackers fingers / Hand. Allows the defender to push the assailant away without much force.

Push away and run.

DO NOT STAY AND FIGHT.

FRONT SINGLE HAND ATTACK/GRAB DEFENSES

1

1. The attacker grabs the wrist or lower arm of defender.

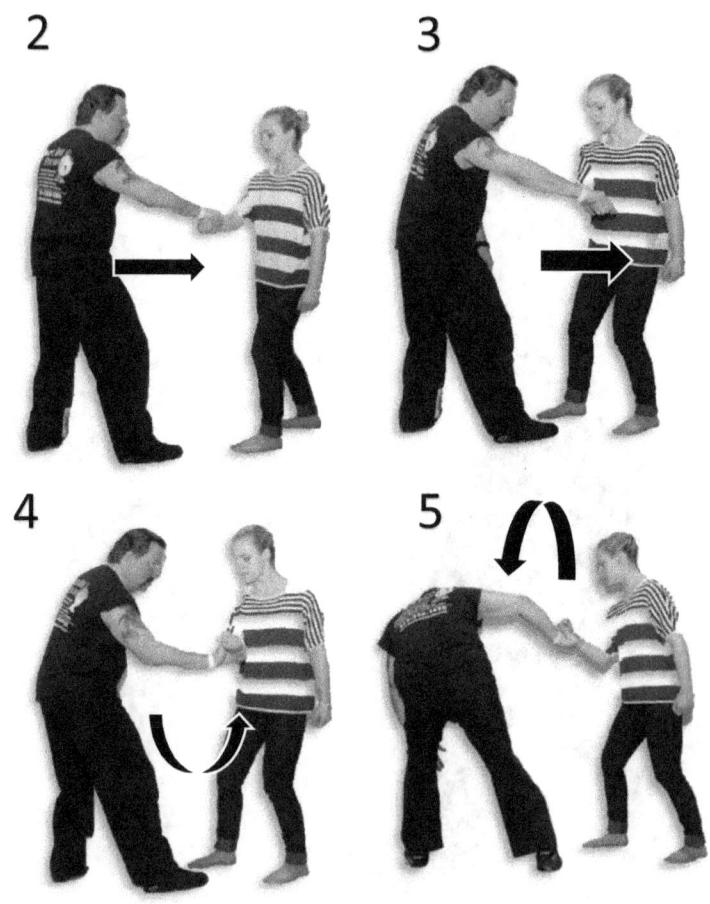

2-5. The defender pulls slightly inward and with a circular motion turns the hand upwards and over.

6

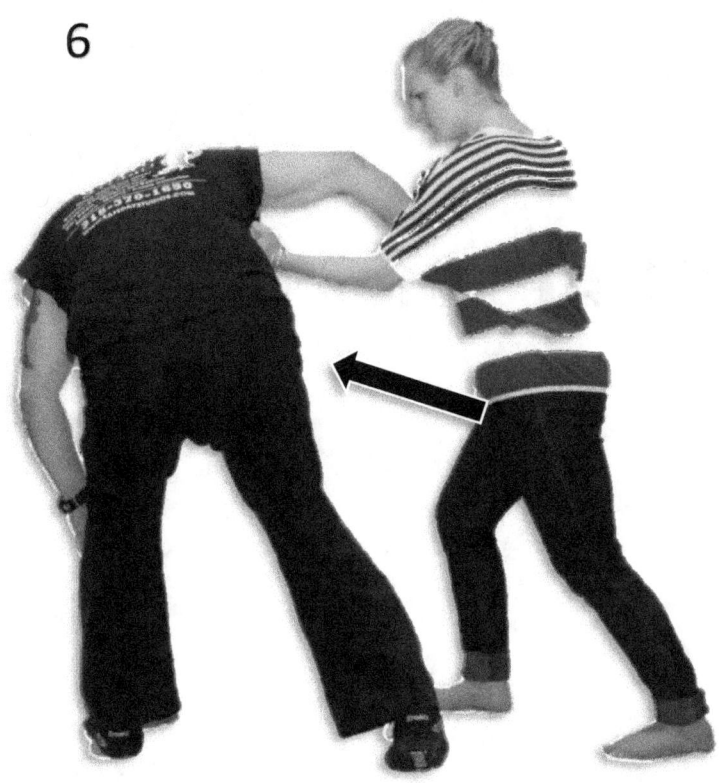

6. The defender can strike the upper ribs or side of attacker hard. Then run away.

DO NOT STAY AND FIGHT

CHAPTER 6

UNDERSTANDING THE IMPACT OF TRAUMA

Trauma-informed care involves a broad understanding of traumatic stress reactions and common responses to trauma. Individuals need to understand how trauma can affect treatment presentation, engagement, and the outcome of behavioral health services. This chapter examines common experiences survivors may encounter immediately following or long after a traumatic experience.

Trauma, including one-time, multiple, or long-lasting repetitive events, affects everyone differently. Some individuals may clearly display criteria associated with posttraumatic stress disorder (PTSD), but many more individuals will exhibit resilient responses or brief subclinical symptoms or consequences that fall outside of diagnostic criteria. The impact of trauma can be subtle, insidious, or outright destructive. How an event affects an individual depends on many factors, including characteristics of the individual, the type and characteristics of the event(s), developmental processes, the meaning of the trauma, and sociocultural factors.

Demonstrating that with an overview of common responses, emphasizing that traumatic stress reactions are normal reactions to abnormal circumstances. It highlights common short- and long-term responses to traumatic experiences in the context of individuals who may seek behavioral health services. This chapter discusses psychological symptoms not represented in the Diagnostic and Statistical Manual of Mental Disorders, Fifth Edition (DSM-5; American Psychiatric Association [APA], 2013a), and responses associated with trauma that either fall below the threshold of mental disorders or reflect resilience. It also addresses common disorders associated with traumatic stress. This chapter explores the role of culture in defining mental illness, particularly PTSD, and ends by addressing co-occurring mental and substance-related disorders.

EFFECTS OF TRAUMA CAUSED BY SEXUAL ASSAULT TEN COMMON EMOTIONAL REACTIONS TO TRAUMA AND THEIR SYMPTOMS

REACTION

A. SHOCK
B. DENIAL
C. CONFUSION
D. HELPLESSNESS
E. FEAR
F. ANGER
G. GUILT
H. SHAME
I. ISOLATION
J. DEPRESSION

SYMPTOMS

A.   Dazed, Robot-like, calm hysteria irrational, has the shakes.

B. Disbelief, demands details, accused of lying, minimizes, memory blocks.

C. Unable to answer simple questions or follow instructions, distortions.

D. Unable to make decisions; Belief of being powerless, loss of autonomy.

E. Trigger response, believes the threat of retaliation, unable to be alone, phobias.

F. Screams, cusses and makes demands, self-destructive acts, hostile directed towards police.

G. Blames self, blames others, believes they caused the assault, "If only" – "I should have" – "Why didn't I/You"

H. Embarrassed to discuss, doesn't want anyone to know, self-condemnation.

I. Withdraws stays in bed, won't talk.

J.   Crying, lethargic, insomnia /hypersomnia, no appetite, lack of personal care, apathetic, CAN EVEN BECOME SUICIDAL.

POINTS TO NOTE

- All victims are likely to experience some, if not all, of these reactions to a certain degree, regardless of the type of assault or their own personal characteristics. Other factors influence the seventy of the impact.

- All of these emotions are normal and are not indications of emotional instability or lack of credibility.

- The stress of these reactions is compounded because the victim does not understand what is happening or what to expect in the future. They need to be told they are normal in an abnormal situation.

- The long-term impact of these reactions can lead to a total inability to function normally, and even to death.

FIVE AREAS OF LIFE, WHICH ARE IMPACTED BY TRAUMA

A. EMOTIONAL

1. Low tolerance for frustration and normal life stresses.

2. Erratic mood swings and irrational reactions.

3. Self-critical, low self-esteem, lack of confidence.

4. Withdrawn, antisocial, paranoid, dependent

5. Long term depression, including suicidal thoughts and acts.

B. PHYSICAL

1. Insomnia/hypersomnia, excessive fatigue.

2. Lack of appetite, insatiable appetite.

3. Headaches, ulcers, backaches, high blood pressure

4 Phantom Pains.

5. Lowered resistance to viruses and disease.

C. COGNITIVE (THINKING)

1. The memory block of the assault

2. Flash Backs dreams, nightmares.

3. An obsessive replay of the assault and what "should"

have been done.

4. Inability to concentrate and/or problem solve.

5. Phobias and generalizations.

D. RELATIONSHIPS

1. Deterioration of current relationships due to the stresses of other reactions. Frequent divorce, (85% of marriages end in divorce within 1 year of an attack)
2. Inability to establish new relationships. Unable to trust.
3. Inability to participate in previously pleasant activities.
4. Frequent mutual blaming, rejection and judgment. Difficulty by all parties in knowing how to be helpful.
5. Difficulty in carrying out normal daily responsibilities, resulting in resentment by others.

E. SEXUALITY

1. Inability to engage in normal sexual relations without memory of the assault.

2. Fear of sex or emotional intimacy.

3. Aversion to all physical touch. Need for excessive body space.

4. Total avoidance of the opposite sex.

5. Promiscuity (sleeps around).

The trauma of sexual assault may have devastating long term emotional and psychological effects... They didn't go away for 37-year-old Rebecca Brown, who died in July ('92) at the same location where she had been raped 19 years earlier.

Rebecca, who was 18 at the time of the assault, had been abducted along with her 11-year-old sister, Amy, by two men in their 20's. The assailants had slashed a tire on Rebecca's car while she and her sister were at a convenience store, and the two men offered to take them home.

SECRETS TO SAFETY

Instead, they drove the two girls 40 miles away from Casper, Wyoming, to the remote Freemont Canyon Bridge above the North Platte River. It was there that Rebecca was brutally raped and beaten and both girls were thrown over the bridge. Amy hit a rock when she fell, killing her.

Rebecca's fall was broken when her hips slammed into a ledge and ricocheted her body into deeper water. Naked from the waist down, with her hip fractured in five places, the following morning she inched herself up a steep rockslide to the road above to seek help.

Natrona County Sheriff Dave Dovala had arrested both abductors the day after the incident. They were convicted and sent to the Wyoming State Prison. Rebecca lived in constant fear they would either escape or be paroled, and she re-lived the incident each time parole was considered. For the two previous years, one of the men had been appealing for a new trial, a fact that had deeply troubled Rebecca. On the day she died, word came the appeal was denied.

We'll never know what was going through her mind in the last few moments of her life, but the events in the hours and weeks before her death might yield some clues. The week before, she bought the movie Ode to Billy Joe, a film about a boy who couldn't cope with memories of being molested by an older man and jumped off Mississippi's Tallahatchie Bridge. She had watched it four times with her boyfriend and cried each time. Having turned to drugs and alcohol soon after the rape, she had been clean and sober for years. She recently had started drinking again.

On the night of her death, she would not tell her boyfriend why she wanted to return to the bridge. He pleaded with her not to go there. The more he pleaded, the faster she drove. With them was her 2-year-old daughter from her failed marriage.

She parked the car to the far side of the bridge and the three walked beside the waist-high railing. Rebecca pointed to where the men had raped her, and where they had thrown her over the bridge. She began re-living the incident again and started to cry. She turned to her boyfriend and said, "I love you" as she ran her fingers through his hair.

He started walking the daughter back to the car so she wouldn't hear her mommy sobbing - that's when they heard the splash of Rebecca's body hitting the water. According to her ex-husband, "she always thought that she should have died and not her sister. I think she was to the point she just gave up."

SECRETS TO SAFETY

Rebecca's ashes were buried on top of Amy's casket at Highland Cemetery in Casper. More than 500 persons attended the funeral. Sheriff Dovala put it this way "she had been raped and murdered 19 years ago, but only died that Friday."

7 CHAPTER

THE AFTER EFFECTS

In a Recent report from Susan Mulligan published by US News and World report in 2017 she noted that victims of sexual assault and rape were far more likely to tell the police of their attacks in 2017 than the previous year, according to a government report, a dramatic development for advocates who have long struggled to convince victims to report such crimes.

The Bureau of Labor Statistics' Criminal Victimization report for 2017 found that incidences of sexual assaults and rapes increased only marginally from 2016 to 2017, from 19.7 per 1,000 residents 12 or older to 20.6 people per 1,000 in 2017. But the reporting of such crimes to police jumped from 23 percent in 2016 to 40 percent the following year.

The report does not explain the jump in reporting. But the numbers suggest that the #MeToo movement, which was coined in 2006 and exploded in 2017 with accusations against very prominent people in entertainment, media and politics, is not merely a social media phenomenon.

"There's definitely been a cultural shift," with sexual assault victims becoming more open about their experiences, says Karen Weiss, a sociology professor at West Virginia University who specializes in crime victimization. "I do think it's good news – the victims (reporting) are the first step. You have to report it to get it into the system," Weiss says.

The increased reporting is not necessarily reflective of victims' heightened confidence in the criminal justice system but rather "a confidence in their ability to be heard," Weiss says.

Rape is the most underreported crime, according to the National Sexual Violence Research Center, and without formal complaints to the police, perpetrators cannot be brought to justice. Sex crimes are among the least likely to result in a prison sentence, according to the Rape,

Abuse & Incest National Network, with few than half of one percent of rapists incarcerated.

It also unleashed a Twitter-led outpouring from women, famous and not, who said they, too, had been the victims of sexual assault and rape. Later, as stories involving decades-old sexual assault allegations against former Senate candidate Roy Moore of Alabama and then-Supreme Court nominee Brett Kavanaugh led people to question why victims waited so long to tell their stories, self-identified victims took to Twitter again. This time, the topic was "why I didn't report," and victims – mostly buy not entirely women – explained the fear and shame that led them to decide not to talk to police.

The timing of the #MeToo movement and the Justice Department report suggest that sexual assault and rape victims were feeling more comfortable going to police even before #MeToo took off. Judd's revelations came in October of 2017.

Its still unlikely sexual assault victims will see their attackers sent behind bars, according to analyses by the Rape, Abuse & Incest National Network, which are drawn from government statistics. But it starts with reporting, Weiss notes.

"Once it's in the system, it's up to the police to do their job and, of course, the prosecutors to take their case," she says. "Things could change with a cultural tidal wave. But it really is going to be up to the institutional response."

TYPES OF SEXUAL ASSAULT

DATE/ACQUAINTANCE RAPE

A.   DEFINITION: Any time a dating partner or acquaintance forces the other person into sexual activity without that person's consent

B.   Accounts for about 75% of all reported sexual assaults.

C.   Offenders are expressing their feelings of anger, power, and/or need to control.

D.   Offenders prefer to know their victims because it allows the opportunity to place the victim in a vulnerable position without alarming the victim. The danger is recognized too late.

E.   Victims of date rape suffer RAPE TRAUMA SYNDROME and have added impact in the areas of guilt, future relationships, fear of retaliation, and judgments from others.

F.   Date rape remains the most frequently under-reported type of sexual assault.

G.   Victims need to be reassured that date rape is a crime, "NO" meant "NO", and the victim did not cause the assault

H.   Continuum of Date/Acquaintance Rape:

MUTUAL   PERSUASION   COERCION   FORCE
(Exploration) (Whining & Begging) (Same or similar) (Rarely
uses a words, more weapon)

1. Clear, assertive, com-
2. One lacks regard
3. Even less regard for
4. May use physical communications;
Both for the other. One the other. One thinks physical
force or knows "NO" means thinks "NO"

"no" means "yes".   Verbal threats.
   "NO".   "Maybe".

SECRETS TO SAFETY

RAPE OF GAY AND LESBIAN VICTIMS

A.   An offender may assault to punish the victim for his/her sexual preference.

B   Some assaults are not related to the victim's sexual orientation, which may be unknown to the offender.

C. Victims rarely report the assault because it will require publicly disclosing their homosexuality.

D.   Homosexual victims suffer RAPE TRAUMA SYNDROME just like anyone else, with added impact in the areas of guilt and relationships.

F.   Rapists of gay men are not necessarily homosexual. Rape of both gay and "straight" men is often very violent and may result in death.

RAPE OF THE ELDERLY

A.   A victim may symbolize an authority figure that the offender wants to control or retaliate against.

B.   79% of the offenders are complete strangers to the victim.

C.   Elderly victims usually live alone, are less able to resist, and suffer greater and more frequent injury.

D.   Victims are unlikely to report the assault due to difficulties with mobility, extreme fear of retaliation, amount of time and energy required to pursue charges, and generational issues of shame and taboo in discussing sexual acts.

E. Offenders frequently are young, white, single males with a history of dysfunctional families and emotional/behavioral problems. Their mood at the time of the assault is typically angry and/or depressed.

F. Most (76%) of the assaults occur in the victim's home.

G. Elderly victims suffer RAPE TRAUMA SYNDROME, with added impact on fear, helplessness, isolation, and shame. They may lose possessions of great sentimental value and ANY financial loss can be economically devastating.

MALE RAPE

A. The dynamics are similar to the rapes of women.

B. 90% of male victims never report the assault to the authorities. 70% Never tell anyone. (Statistics from surveys of offenders and anonymous surveys of male adults.)

C. 60% of male rape cases involve kidnap, burglary, and/or robbery.

D. The victim is usually in his late teens/early 20's.

E. Single assailants usually rely on a weapon. Multiple assailants, on the other hand, generally rely on the sheer force of numbers. This may be due to the offenders' anticipation of a struggle, or maybe because they derive more pleasure in brutalizing a male victim.

Consequently, this may indicate a sadistic tendency in men-on-men assaults.

F. Sodomy (anal intercourse) is the most frequent form of sexual assault on men

G. Male rapists are not necessarily homosexual, although very few also rape women.

H. The majority of victims and offenders are offenders are of the same ethnic, racial and economic group.

I. Men suffer RAPE TRAUMA SYNDROME but often find it more difficult to express the trauma reactions other than anger or aggression. They suffer added impact in the areas of guilt for not being able to resist, shame, and concerns about being homosexual. Men tend to be more comfortable talking with another man.

OFFENDER PROFILES

MYTHS and FACTS Regarding Sexual Assault OFFENDERS

A. MYTH: Sex offenders are dirty old men.

B. MYTH: Sex offenders are usually violent and brutal.

C. MYTH: Sex offenders are ugly and can't attract women.

D. MYTH: Sex offenders are crazy.

E. MYTH: All sex offenders hate their mothers.

F. MYTH: Once a sex offender Always a sex offender.

A. FACT: Sex offenders come from all socioeconomic backgrounds and usually begin assaults in their adolescence.

B. FACT: The majority of offenders do NOT physical injure their victims. The assault is most frequently accomplished through the use of force or threat

C. FACT: Sex offenders come in either package attractive or ugly. Most have been married and have children.

D. FACT: Only 5% of all convicted sex offenders are diagnosed as psychotic or sociopathic. They do, however, have very serious emotional problems which result in dangerous behavior.

E. FACT: Some sex offenders had abusive mothers. However, sexually aggressive behavior is the result of a complicated combination of family background, thinking disorders, and life stresses. Although more than 50% of offenders were sexually abused as children, most of their perpetrators were men.

F. FACT: A study conducted on sex offenders will become repeat offenders showed that in the Texas prison system at least 70% will repeat, but a study in Oregon reported only 10% will repeat. However, a 4-year recidivism rate of incarceration alone is a poor deterrent and does not cure. Psychological counseling has shown some positive results, but some experts believe there is no complete cure.

METHODS OF ASSAULT

A.   CON, TRICK, or COERCE
1. Uses verbal and psychological manipulation.
2. Most common in date and acquaintance rape.

B.   SURPRISE
1. Selects victim and follows or lays in wait
2. Uses the threat of force, overwhelms the victim with fear.

C.   BLITZ
1. Initiates assault with a violent attack.
2.   Uses physical force to overpower/incapacitate the victim.

FOUR CLASSIFICATIONS OF ADULT SEX OFFENDERS:

(There are many variations and sub-categories. These are broad general classifications, shown in order from least common to most common. Offenders often are mixtures of these categories.)

A. OPPORTUNISTIC Rapist:

1. Takes advantage of the situation during the commission of another crime.

2. Typically has been drinking or doing drugs.

3. Uses minimal force or threat.

4. Arrest record will reflect the crime he was originally committing.

5. Typically is NOT a repeat sexual assault offender.

B. SADISTIC Rapist:
1. Aggression and violence are eroticized.

2. The act is symbolic of destruction/elimination. The victim is symbolic of a person the offender wants to destroy.

3. Assault is calculated and pre-planned. Brings weapons.

149

4. Assault is ritualistic, involves bondage, torture, and bizarre sex acts.

5. The offender is verbally commanding and degrading.

6. Assault is of extended duration with repeated assaults.

7. Injuries are inflicted to sexual areas of the body. In extreme cases, the victim is murdered and mutilated.

8. Offenders are usually in the 30's but begin fantasizing of rape and murder at a young age.

9. Obsessed with sadism and masochism (S & M), bondage and snuff pornography.

10. Bondage is neat, symmetrical, and various types are used.

11. Collects sexual devices and brings them to the assault.

C. ANGER Rapist:
1. Wants to assert his masculinity or punish and degrade. Is angry at life and blames women. Sex is a

weapon and assault are an attempt to get even or take what he is owed.

2. Uses BLITZ approach. More force than necessary is used to overpower the victim. Injuries are frequent and may accidentally kill the victim.

3. Offender's mood is angry or depressed. Language is abusive and obscene.

4. Assault is relative to short duration.

5. The victim is selected for availability, usually strangers. The victim is at the "wrong place at the wrong time".

6. The offender is frequently impotent and may use devices.

7. Assaults are spontaneous and sporadic. Rage is released and it takes time and/or new precipitating event to build up again.

D. POWER Rapist:

1. Wants to prove his masculinity. Assaults are an attempt to control and sexually control the victim to feel adequate.

2. Uses a CON or SURPRISE approach. Uses force or threat to overcome resistance. Once in control, may lay down the weapon. The offender may accidentally injure the victim.

3. Offender's mood is anxious. Language is inquisitive and instructional. The offender may ask the victim for praise or reassurance.

4. Assault may be of extended duration, holding victim captive for a lengthy period of time.
5. The victim is selected for specific characteristics, and availability. Offender normally will choose a victim in the same age range.

6. Assault is premeditated and includes persistent rape fantasies of the victim being unable to resist the actor. May follow and/or watch victim for a long time until the right opportunity to approach. Offender masturbates to fantasies.

7. Offenses are obsessive and repetitive. Aggression may increase over time as reality never measures up to the fantasy, and frustration grows. The offender may assault once a week.

8. Frequently commits date and acquaintance rapes. The offender is usually known as a "nice guy" who likes to hang out in bars.

9. Often apologizes after an assault and may nurse victim's injuries. The offender may stay and talk or ask the victim for a date. Usually describes the victim as "consenting."

SECRETS TO SAFETY

CHAPTER **8**

STAGES OF ADJUSTMENT

Each person going through a crisis of any kind progresses through stages of emotional adjustment. A victim may spend a great deal of time in one stage and only touch lightly on another or may pass through a number of the stages over and over again, each time experiencing them with a different intensity. Furthermore, anyone close to the victim may experience these stages as well.

Emotional, psychological and physical issues arise after the acts of sexual assault or rape to most victims. Many different issues may occur, but specific psychological ones may leave an impact on the life of those affected. It is important to know what these problems may be, how to cope with them and how to resolve or repair the damage.

Lasting effects of these crimes may impact victims in various ways. Rape Trauma Syndrome otherwise known as Sexual Assault Trauma Syndrome is a psychological impairment that a rape or sexual assault victim may encounter after the crimes have been committed. This syndrome often disrupts normal physical, emotional, intellectual, behavioral and social characteristics and behaviors of the affected person.

SIGNS OF SEXUAL ASSAULT TRAUMA SYNDROME

This type of trauma has characteristic symptoms that may warn others that the victim is going through this issue. Common psychological and physical warning signs may appear. The acts of rape often leave lasting damage, and this specific issue may show up during the trauma, just after the act has occurred or sometimes even years later. This is typically seen in women because they have become the majority victim of these crimes. However, men have been observed experiencing this issue when sexual abuse occurred when they were a child or into their teenage years.

Stage One: Initial Shock

Shock following an assault can take on many forms. You may experience emotional as well as physical shock, which could be exhibited in controlled and withdrawn behavior, or highly expressive behavior such as crying, screaming, or shaking. You may not be comfortable expressing these feelings to others.

Stage Two: Denial

Also called pseudo-adjustment, this stage may find you attempting to go on with your normal routine, wanting to forget about the assault. This denial or rationalization of what happened is an attempt to deal with inner turmoil and return to normal life.

Stage Three: Reactivation

This stage involves a re-experiencing of the feelings from Stage One, usually brought on by the triggering of memories of the assault. Feelings of depression, anxiety and shame may increase. Other symptoms can include nightmares, flashbacks, a sense of vulnerability, mistrust and physical complaints.

Stage Four: Anger

You may experience feelings of anger—often toward yourself, friends, significant others, society, the legal system, all men/women, etc. With skillful support this anger can be redirected in ways that are healing.

Stage Five: Integration (Closure)

As you integrate the thoughts and feelings stemming from the assault into your life experience you will begin to feel "back on track." As a result of support, education, and the passing of time, you will feel strengthened.

Help Healing From Trauma

After experiencing a traumatic event, such as a sexual assault, you might find yourself reacting to situations in ways you would not have before the assault. You may feel numb, like the whole world is just floating by. Or, you may have memories that are so strong you find it difficult to stay in the present moment. These strong memories are called flashbacks, and they can be triggered by a thought, smell, color, or anything that reminds you of the attack.

If you have a flashback, try grounding yourself and reentering the present moment using sensory techniques.

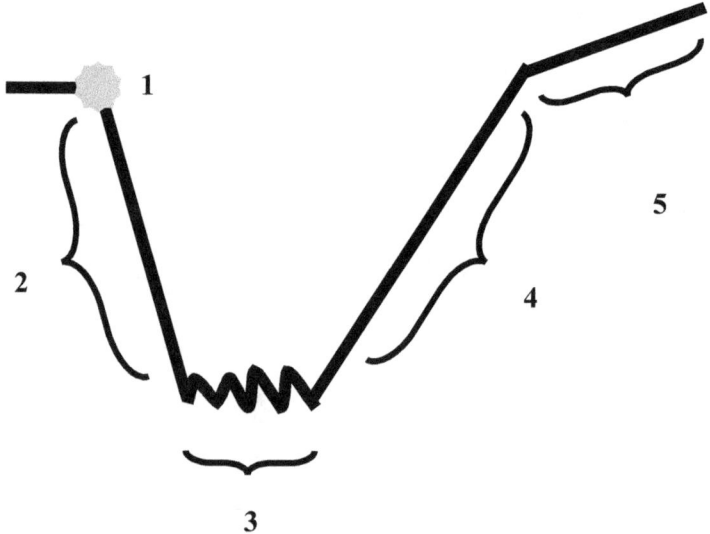

1. Critical Incident (Assault)
2. Immediate Drop (change) in personality.
3. Stages of Adjustment (shock, denial, anger, bargaining, depression, may spend a great deal of time in one stage and only touch lightly on another, or may pass through a number of the stages over and over again)
4. Stages of Recovery (acceptance and assimilation).
5. Stages of Healing (growth).

Acute stages of this trouble are often recognized within a short time after criminal acts have occurred. This may be days, weeks, or in some instance's years. Typical behavior responses may not be observed, but most follow a particular pattern. Hysterical or agitated behavior often arises during this stage with crying spells suffered by the victim to include anxiety attacks. Controlled reactions of denial from the acts may occur, or victims may not be able to recall what transpired. Often the victims of these crimes are reserved with an outward calm. They appear unaffected, but the inner turmoil often bursts forth through these stages.

When disorientation does not appear in the acute stages, hysteria, befuddlement, anxiety that paralyzes, nausea, a numbness of emotion or obsessions with bathing and cleaning their body may follow some of the initial symptoms.

The outward adjustment stage follows the acute stage when survivors are ready to move forward. This phase of the syndrome appears as a readjustment to normal routine living. However, these individuals struggle with extreme turmoil on the inside. Various types of behavior may be viewed when these persons attempt to cope with the crimes affecting them. Often, they will act as if nothing happened and attempt to return to daily life. Others refuse to discuss anything and may even withdraw from others to varying degrees. Some decide to alter their physical appearance or pack up and move to another area.

During these initial stages, a myriad of symptoms may arise. Deterioration of health, ongoing anxiety issues, helplessness or extreme mood swings are often additional issues that arise at any point during these stages. Women victims are frequently the bearers of exceptional anger and hostility compared to the male survivors. After memories resurface or during denial stages, flashbacks of the rape or sexual assault activities may appear. Recurring nightmares often disturb sleeping patterns or insomnia will affect those with persistent fear of the crime.

During renormalization, victims often are aware that they are adjusting in phases to the trauma. The impact of the sexual assault or rape is identified for those in denial, and any supplementary damage is discovered through any coping tactics that were used. Women who survive these crimes frequently seek therapeutic treatment much sooner than their male counterparts. When men suffer through these acts, they usually wait an extensive period before any type of therapy or psychological treatment is sought. A study revealed the average interval after damage occurred to obtain therapy is a stretch of just over sixteen years for male victims.

Personal relationships after sexual assault or rape are often the hardest to repair, especially for opposite sex relationships. Keeping and maintaining lasting close relationships is often troublesome for victims. Constant fear of surroundings or panic attacks often occur after the syndrome stages have completed. Abuse of alcohol or drugs and self-mutilation are often coping mechanisms. Some develop phobias or intense fear related to the events that took place. Trust is often elusive for these individuals, but additional therapy may be required for a more permanent resolution.

SECRETS TO SAFETY

ABOUT THE AUTHOR

OFFICER ALVIN GOLDIE MACK Ph.D.

D r. Alvin (Goldie) Mack Jr. Ph.D. is a 10th-degree black belt in Kenpo Karate; he is a tournament competitor, an author & actor.

Dr. Mack has study martial arts since 1968. He holds black belts in Kenpo, Shotokan and Tae Kwon Do, but since 1973 he has centered his attention on the Ed Parker Kenpo System. To this day, he continues to teach Ed Parker's Kenpo System. He was the undefeated Lightweight Champion of Europe from 1974-1976. He was the recipient of the Presidential Sports Award (1977), and Grand Champion of the U.S. Golden Karate Championships (1977).

He was also awarded the Best Sportsman Award at the MARS National Championships (1978). Winner of the 11th Annual Rocky Mountain Nations (1979), the Grand Open Champion of the Southwest Open, Lightweight Division (1980); and was voted a Top Ten Instructor by the Indian Karate Association (1980).

Dr. Mack has been inducted into the Karate's Who's Who Hall of Fame in 1982 and 2018. In 2007 he was inducted into the U.S.A. Martial Arts Hall of Fame as Instructor of the year and School of the year, the Battle of Atlanta Officials Hall of Fame as Referee/Official of the year, the US Martial Arts Hall of Fame as Master Instructor. He was appointed Team Coach of the US National Team at the Good Will Games held in Honolulu, Hawaii February 14–19 2008 and appointed Alliance State Director for the state of Texas January 2008.

Dr. Mack received his Doctorate of Martial Arts Philosophy on February 17, 2008, & Martial Arts Science on July 1, 2009, from the University of Asian Martial Arts Studies and was inducted into the U.S. Martial Arts Hall of Fame (for the second time in two years) Distinguished Master of the Year on August 2, 2008 in Nashville, TN, the Masters Hall of Fame in Anaheim, Cal. on August 16, 2008, and was inducted into the Action Martial Arts Magazine Hall of Fame on January 10, 2009. Dr. Mack was once again inducted into the U.S.A. Martial Arts Hall of Fame (Golden Life Time Achievement Award) on June 20. 2009, Masters Hall of Fame (Life Time Achievement Award) on August 8, 2009, Inducted into the International Independent Martial Arts Association Hall of Fame as Sifu of The Year March 14, 2010 in Port St Joe, Florida, was nominated for induction as "Humanitarian of The Year" for the 2010 U.S.A. Martial Arts Hall of Fame "Hall of Heroes" on May 8th 2010 in Los Angeles, CA, nominated for induction into the World Karate Union Hall of Fame as "Master Self-Defense Instructor of the Year" to be held in New York City, New York on June 26, 2010 and was inducted into the United

States Martial Arts Hall of Fame on July 31, 2010 in Nashville, Tennessee. He was the President of the USA Martial Hall of Fame from 2013 to 2017. Dr. Mack served as a Police Officer in Texas and as a Deputy Sheriff in Kansas. For two years he was a member of the President's Homeland Security Anti-Terrorism Police Task Force. He has conducted over 200-300 anti-rape seminars across the nation annually for the past 20 plus years.

Dr. Alvin Mack is the author of "The Technical training Instructor's Course," a methods text for martial arts, and of a number of training courses.

Mack has worked as an extra on the following films: Blade & Blade II, Necessary Roughness, True Friends, Pearl Harbor, and Shaft. He has also appeared in the following TV series Walker Texas Ranger (1990-2001), Sons of Thunder and The President's Man as a stuntman and featured extra.

SECRETS TO SAFETY

LETTERS OF RECOMMENDATION

O ver the years Dr. Mack has been recognized as a true community leader and an outstanding Police office by several official persons. Forward are many letters of recommendations and noted officials that state unequivocally about Alvin Mack's career   and outstanding record of service to others.

166

HOME INVASION PROTECTION
AND PERSONAL DEFENSE

SENATOR MIKE MONCRIEF

The Senate Chamber
Austin 78711

Committees:

Finance
Health & Human Services
Intergovernmental Relations
Administration, Vice Chair
Redistricting, Ethics & Elections
Sunset Commission
Legislative Health & Human
   Services Oversight Board

November 28, 1994

Alvin D. Mack Jr.
Universal Martial Arts Acadamy
 & Training Center
1325 E. Abrams St. Suite A
Arlington, Texas   76010

Dear Alvin:

Thank you for your recent letter regarding your program involving your martial arts acadamy.

You are to be commended for your dedication and hardwork in focusing your efforts on "prevention" rather than addressing the issue "after the fact." This approach demonstrates creativity and innovation which are both vital to a successful program.

Good luck with program and I look forward to hearing more about it in the future.

Sincerely,

Mike Moncrief
MJM/br

AUSTIN OFFICE
P.O. BOX 12068, AUSTIN, TEXAS 78711   (512) 463-0112   FAX (512) 463-0326   TEXAN 255-0112   TDD (512) 476-3758
DISTRICT OFFICE
1701 RIVER RUN RD., SUITE 302, BOX 18, FORT WORTH, TEXAS 76107   (817) 338-0420   FAX (817) 338-9362   METRO (817) 429-3524

TARRANT COUNTY
Judge Charles Griffin Poly Sub-Courthouse
3212 Miller Avenue
Fort Worth, Texas 76119
817-531-5625

SIDNEY THOMPSON
JUSTICE OF THE PEACE
PRECINCT 8

November 30, 1994

Mr. Alvin D Mack
Universal Martial Arts Academy
1325 E Abrams St. Ste A
Arlington, Texas 76010

Dear Mr. Mack:

It is my pleasure to write in support of the University Martial
Arts Academy and Training Center. Your efforts in this program will
be greatly appreciated. It is nice to have someone in the Community
who still cares about our youth. If there is anything that I can
do to keep this Academy a success, please feel free to call me
anytime at (817)531-5627.

Respectfully,

Judge Sidney Thompson
Justice of the Peace
Precinct #8

To A.D. Mack
Justice for all,

FORMER US ATTORNEY GENERAL JANET RENO

SECRETS TO SAFETY

City of Arlington Texas

Elzie Odom
Councilman
District 1

Home (Metro 817) 274-8049

December 6, 1994

Mr. Alvin D. Mack, Jr.
Universal Martial Arts Academy
 & Training Center
1325 E. Abram St., Suite A
Arlington, TX 76010

Dear Alvin:

It was my pleasure to have toured your facilities, and reviewed your existing and proposed programs on November 30, 1994. I enjoyed visiting with you.

I commend you on your commitment, dedication and desire to help troubled youth and battered women of our society. Your ability as a karate instructor and your law enforcement background has prepared you for this kind of dedicated endeavor. I especially commend you for being a father and yet willing to reach out to others.

I sincerely hope that your "leap of faith" to establish your training center will receive the support of all who support your goals of improving our community and enhancing the future of our children.

If I can ever be of assistance, please advise.

Sincerely,

Elzie Odom
District One - Council member

EO/db

MARTIN FROST
24th District, Texas

RULES COMMITTEE

HOUSE ADMINISTRATION
COMMITTEE

FLOOR WHIP

WASHINGTON OFFICE
2459 Rayburn House Office Building
Washington, DC 20515
(202) 225-3605

Congress of the United States
House of Representatives
Washington, DC 20515

November 4, 1994

Mr. Alvin Mack
Chief Instructor
Universal Martial Arts Academy and Training Center
1325 E. Abrams St, Suite A
Arlington, Texas 76010

Dear Mr. Mack:

It is my pleasure to write in support of the Universal Martial Arts Academy and Training Center (UMAATC), which has provided free programs for at risk youth and families to insure that no one is left out due to their inability to pay.

Our community continues to have a shocking number of young people dropping out of school and becoming involved with gang activity and drugs. The UMAATC has afforded our community and its participants a fighting chance to become productive citizens. This organization has established community leadership and is committed to serving the low income population which has a high occurrence of gang activity and drugs.

Again, I congratulate your efforts, and I urge you to continue the work in our community. If I may be of further assistance, please do not hesitate to contact me.

Sincerely,

MARTIN FROST
Member of Congress

MF:lcw

SECRETS TO SAFETY

TEXAS FOMER GOVERNOR ANN RICHARDS

RAY BAILY HUTCHINSON FORMER MAYOR OF DALLAS
FORMER CONGRESSWOMEN